THE
DAWN
OF A
NEW ERA
IN SYRIA

THE
DAWN
OF A
NEW ERA
IN SYRIA

MARGARET MCGILVARY

FIRST PUBLISHED IN 1920
BY FLEMING H. REVELL COMPANY, NEW YORK

Garnet
PUBLISHING

THE DAWN OF A NEW ERA IN SYRIA

Published by
Garnet Publishing Limited
8 Southern Court
South Street
Reading
RG1 4QS
UK

This edition copyright © Garnet Publishing, 2001

New edition 2001
First published in 1920 by Fleming H. Revell Company, New York

ISBN 1 85964 167 9

British Library Cataloguing-in-Publication Data
A catalogue record for this book is available from the British Library.

Printed in Lebanon

Jacket illustration by Janette Hill

Preface

MANY of our favourite books have been written "by request." A little boy once said to a famous author, "If you will write me a book about animals, my father will print it." The result was the "Just So Stories."

It is impossible to estimate how many people have sought out the American residents in Syria with questions in regard to their experiences during the war. Newspaper reporters, directors of relief-campaigns, and agents of political propaganda have been clamouring for stories, for statistics, for facts pertinent to this or that particular issue. It is evident that America is interested in Syria, and those of us who are concerned with Syria's welfare feel that we can do her no greater service than to introduce her to the American public. Geographically this land is regarded in America as a "remote corner of the globe," and perhaps there are comparatively few at home who realize the numerous ties which bind the United States to this small land on the eastern coast of the Mediterranean. American philanthropy has been pouring millions of dollars of American money into Syria during the last five years. Moreover, within the last nine months the question has arisen of an intimate

7

political relationship between the two countries. If this little volume answers any questions, and succeeds in arousing an interest in this struggling nation, it will amply fulfil its purpose.

I have been greatly handicapped by the fact that for years there has been no comprehensive treatise on Syria. If I may judge by my own scanty information before I came here to live, the average American knows very little of the geography, the government, the economy of the country, its wartime experiences, or its present problems. Any book on Syria, however simple, must supply these deficiencies. For this reason I have been forced to treat certain subjects more in detail than would otherwise have been necessary.

"Ambassador Morgenthau's Story" is the only authoritative work on Turkey during the war that has been published. I purposely refrained from reading this book until I had completed my own, as I wished to avoid influence upon my point of view. In one or two instances I have verified my information by referring to his discussion of such technicalities as the Capitulations, but in all such cases I have cited Mr. Morgenthau as my authority. If there are other points of similarity, it is purely accidental.

I am under special obligation to my uncle and my aunt, Mr. and Mrs. Charles A. Dana; and but for their encouragement and generous interest I doubt whether I should have had the courage to undertake the task. Mrs. Dana has given me invaluable assistance in the preparation of certain chapters on subjects where her information was more complete than mine. Mr. Dana has allowed me free use of records of Press-work and relief-activities and has set no limit to my use of facts regarding certain of his personal experiences which have been little known outside of our family circle.

I am also indebted to my uncle, Lewis Bayles Paton, Professor in Hartford Theological Seminary, Hartford, Connecticut, for revising the manuscript and reading proof.

M. McG.

'Aleih, Lebanon.

Contents

Contents 13

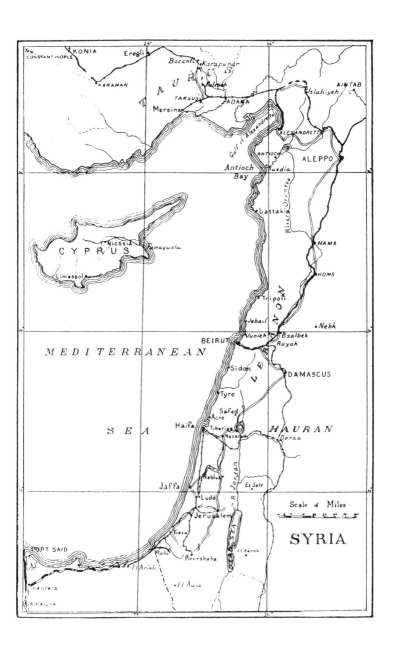

II

THE CLOSING OF A HIGHWAY OF THE NATIONS

SYRIA was perhaps the most completely isolated country in the world during the Great War. As the result of an almost ironical series of circumstances this land which for so many centuries played such an important rôle in history was for practically four years hidden behind a drawn curtain. This "bridge of the world," as it is sometimes called, this highway between Asia and Africa for the conquests and commerce of nations, became for the first time in recorded history as much out of touch with the trend of world events as the bleak plains of Patagonia, or Lapland.

The history of Syria is in itself practically a résumé of the history of civilization from its earliest beginnings to the present day. The Turkish Empire as it existed before this last great war included areas which were more richly endowed with the heritage of the past than any other portions of the world's surface. Mesopotamia probably cradled the earliest civilization. Egypt contains the richest and best-preserved records of a highly developed ancient culture. Arabia and Syria, both former Turkish provinces, gave birth to the three great religions of the world, Islâm, Judaism, and

Christianity. Jerusalem is the shrine of all these religions, and Moslem, Jew and Christian jostle each other in the narrow streets of the Holy City and contest with fanatical hatred for the ownership of the places that are sacred to all three sects alike. The name of this remote and crumbling Oriental city is familiar to " people and realms of every tongue," and the ignorant Russian peasant who has scarcely heard of Moscow and Petrograd is nevertheless hoarding his savings for a pilgrimage to Jerusalem.

The historian, the Bible student, the archæologist, the statesman must all include within their professional equipment a comprehension of the history of Syria and its problems. In some respects Syria is the most backward country in the world, and might almost be regarded as an exhibit in the museum of time. A large majority of the peasant population of the Holy Land to-day cultivate their soil and conduct their social life just as their ancestors did three thousand years and more ago. Many of the agricultural implements and the household utensils have not been altered in the slightest particular from those which are described in the Bible. Old tribal customs, especially among the Jews, still prevail, and the traveller is constantly impressed with a sense of unreality as if he were observing animated tableaux illustrating a long-loved book as he sees at every turn the episodes of Biblical history reproduced in the life of the modern inhabitants of the " Bible-land."

In this respect Syria is the land " where all things always seem the same "; and yet, on the other hand,

Syria is the one spot still left on the face of the earth with which the world-peace settlement has not yet been able to cope. It was a comparatively easy problem for the Entente to agree upon the terms under which Germany and Austria should be reinstated; but one item of the docket with which the Conference must deal before its work is finished promises endless difficulties, and may even sow the seeds of discord between the parties of the Entente. That item is the disposal of Syria. The searchlight of the world is turned in Syria's direction. There are a score of conflicting and powerful political forces at work, and the task of evolving an equitable solution from the chaos of greed bids fair to prove well-nigh impossible. To the mind of the Jews the hour has sounded for their reëstablishment in the land of which they were centuries ago despoiled. For the Arabs the time has come to assert their claims over the vast territory which is theirs by right of prevailing race and language. The Syrians are clamouring for independence. England and France and Italy have each political or commercial aspirations which make the possession of Syria highly desirable, and America stands in that awkward position of being the sponsor of Syria's choice, an invitation which she cannot disregard in view of the famous " Fourteen Points."

However much the existence of Syria had to be reckoned with by the various combatants in the conflict, its real internal life during the war was practically unknown to the world. Outsiders saw in the newspapers little mention of other than military events in Syria. Some may have been stirred by appeals to help the starving Syrians, but how many realized that the suffering was not due entirely to the exigencies of war but to the deliberate attempt of the rulers to exterminate a subject race? Those within the country felt themselves growing almost daily further out of touch with the march of world events. The great majority of these also realized that they were prisoners who faced both indignity and starvation. In one sense, all who remained in Syria during the war, whether voluntarily or otherwise, were prisoners. Foreigners and Syrians alike found themselves fettered by lack of funds, materials, ways and means; by government regulations and interference; and they were in danger of mental stagnation, and even death from disease, famine or torture. Those were very dark hours. Like a night during sickness they dragged on, and it seemed that the dawn would never break.

In Roman times Syria was the granary of the world which encircled the Mediterranean, and she is still capable of producing wheat to feed that little world. Yet in our day, during the reign of a few Turkish governors, some of whom were eminently suited to the worst Roman era, one-half the population of Syria was wiped out entirely through disease and starvation. Even Belgium and Serbia, which probably suffered as heavily as any of the small countries engaged in the war, cannot show as high a percentage of mortality due to these causes.

Probably no part of the world contained also in so small an area representatives of so many nationalities as did Syria at the beginning of the war. Her internal life, therefore, during the war presented not only the problems of her Syrian inhabitants, a race subject at that time to the Sultan of Turkey, but also certain peculiar features in relation to the foreign residents. The vicissitudes of the latter, as seen by the writer of this book, form a part of the story which cannot be lightly told.

These pages are written in Lebanon during the peaceful summer of 1919; and although the surroundings are identical with those in which the events of the war occurred, everything has been so altered since the British occupation less than a year ago that we sometimes wonder whether it was a dream after all. We use the words " during the war " as if we were referring to an epoch which we can only dimly remember. So rapidly does one adjust oneself to new conditions!

I came out to Syria in the spring of 1914, having just graduated from college, to work as secretary to my uncle, Mr. Charles A. Dana, Manager of the American Mission Press in Beirût. The offer particularly tempted me for I understood that life in Syria was peculiarly rich and delightful, affording many opportunities for travel in the Near East. Moreover, as a point of contact with the outside world it could scarcely be equalled. "Everybody that is anybody " eventually visits the Holy Land, just as every one visits Paris; but in Beirût, unlike a great city like Paris, the small American community is privileged to entertain and become well acquainted with the distinguished guests who are constantly passing. Since one must always behold the greater part of the world in a mirror, it seemed to me there was no better place than Syria for a Lady of Shalott.

I had been in Syria only four months when the war began, and I then discovered that I had chosen as my residence for the next two years and eight months the most out-of-the-way corner of the world, instead of the greatest highway.   However, life there held ample recompense for its isolation.   In my position at the American Press I was in constant touch with the problems of relief-work, and I came to know and love the land and the people in a way that is possible only in a community which is cut off from the rest of the world.

I have incorporated into this book some sections of reports of the Beirût Chapter of the American National Red Cross which, as secretary of that organization from 1914 to 1917, it was my task to prepare for the main office in Washington.

In the fall of 1917 Mr. Dana was deported from Beirût, owing to the hostility of the Turkish Governor, Azmi Bey; and the Dana family, including myself, spent the last year of the war—one of many downs and ups—in Constantinople, returning to Beirût in the spring of 1919.

At the beginning of the Great War Beirût was the third city of the Ottoman Empire, a flourishing port with an extensive trade.   Though it has no great historical past like Damascus, its story is not lacking in interest.   It was an ancient Phœnician settlement, and as such enjoyed a flourishing trade with Egypt, Tarshish, and the Greek islands.   It eventually passed under Roman control, which marked the beginning of the most prosperous period of its history. After its capture by the Arabs in 635 A. D. it remained Moslem until 1111, when Count Baldwin took it for Christendom. In 1187 it was recaptured by Ṣalâḥ-ed-dîn (Saladin), and has since then been nominally under Moslem rule, although for one period of many years it was the seat of the rebel government of the Druze Emir, Fakhreddîn. From that time on until comparatively recent years, whoever its nominal rulers have been, it has been under the influence of the Druze Emirs of Lebanon. In October, 1918, it was recaptured a second time for Christianity by the Egyptian Expeditionary Force under General Sir Edmund Allenby.

Never in all this history of capture and recapture has Beirût been so isolated from the rest of the world as during the past four years. The neighbouring coast city of Jebail, the ancient Gebal, was besieged by the Assyrians, but was in constant touch with Egypt during the whole siege; Tyre was besieged fifteen years by Alexander, and still maintained her sea-trade. Yet in our day not only the coast cities, but the whole of Syria was utterly cut off from the outside world and was the victim of disease, of starvation, and of tyranny.

Syria from its location is naturally a highway. Generally outlined, it occupies the entire coast of the most eastern extremity of the Mediterranean. It extends from the Taurus Mountains, which border Asia Minor, to Egypt and the Arabian Desert, and inland to Mesopotamia. All traffic from the coasts of Asia Minor must pass through its northern portion. Xenophon's Ten Thousand filed through the Cilician Gates into Syria on their march toward Mesopotamia in the days of the younger Cyrus, just as did the troops of Von der Goltz on their expedition to Bagdad. Hittites, Assyrians and Egyptians centuries ago met and clashed in Syria, for it was the roadway to and from their respective kingdoms. North of Beirût the deep gorge of the Dog River affords one of the easiest passes from the coast into the heart of Lebanon. Assyrians, Babylonians, Hittites, Egyptians, Greeks and Romans have all passed that way. Near the mouth of the river the cliffs are covered with inscriptions in almost every tongue known to antiquity cut into the solid rock, some so worn by time that one can scarcely distinguish the queer, antique figures, others remarkably well preserved. Napoleon III left his tablet there. The most glorious and most recent inscription is that of General Sir Edmund Allenby, placed there soon after the British occupation of Beirût.

In recent years Syria has become of strategic value as the one connecting link between the capital of the Turkish Empire and its most easternly provinces, as well as its nominal dependency, Egypt. Germany recognized this and knew also that by maintaining the Bagdad Railway and her colonies in Palestine she could always menace any possible concession to England for a railroad which would carry mail and trade by the shortest possible route from Europe to Persia and India.

When the war began the first step in the separation of Syria from the world was the severance of connec-

tion with Egypt, which cast in her lot with the Entente
by declaring herself independent of Turkey. Next
came the cessation of maritime commerce as one by one
the European countries broke relations with the Ottoman Empire; and, six months after Turkey herself
entered the war, scarcely a ship was seen save an occasional distant French or British cruiser patrolling the
coast. Then Mesopotamia fell into the hands of the
British; but, as a wide desert separated that part of
Asia from Syria, no military advance was made beyond Bagdad, and no connection existed between the
British army and the eastern border of Syria. There
remained only the slender thread of the railway which
connected Syria with the government at Constantinople. This was controlled by the Turks and the Germans; hence Syria, cut off on three sides, was at the
mercy of her hostile rulers and their equally hostile
allies who held the fourth side.

Germany cared nothing for Syria save as a possible future German colony and as a buffer against
Egypt. The Turkish Government bore no love for its
province whose Arab and Syrian population was
frankly disaffected. Germany encouraged the isolation of Syria as a whole in order to further her larger
schemes which included the complete disintegration of
the Ottoman Empire. Turkey seized the opportunity
to vent her barbaric instincts and to harass and murder
a nation she hated, and in order to accomplish this she
closed every possible door to outside help through the
mails or otherwise. For these reasons, Turkey was
cut off from all save her allies; and had Bulgaria not

entered the war on the side of the Central Powers, the Ottoman Empire would have been completely encircled by enemies, and would soon have fallen into the power of the Entente. As it was, Syria became, partly by force of circumstances, and partly through concerted action, completely isolated.

Those four years when Syria was entirely segregated from the rest of the world formed the blackest period of her history. Just as the darkest hours precede the dawn, and in sickness the vitality is at lowest ebb in the early morning hours and the pulse weakens like a candle flickering in the wind, so the flame of Syria's national life was scarcely sustained. When dawn came at last, it found Syria very weak but still alive, and ready and eager to face a new future.

II

THE DISINTEGRATION OF SYRIA

NO small part of the difficulties in Syria during the war was due to the fact that she was at the mercy of the Turk so far as her one connection with the outside world was concerned, and this largely because of the form of government. Turkey changed in 1908 from an absolute to a constitutional monarchy governed by the Sultan and a parliament consisting of delegates from the various provinces. As a matter of fact, between 1915 and 1918 a large number of these delegates never reached Constantinople, or, if there, were so out of touch with their constituents that there was little representation in the true sense of the term. The real power rested in the hands of the Committee of Union and Progress which had smothered the ambitions of the Young Turk Party that had aspired to at least a nominally liberal government, and which controlled the Sultan, the Cabinet, Parliament and the majority of the provincial governors. The Triumvirate of the Committee of Union and Progress were Talaat Pasha, Minister of the Interior; Enver Pasha, Minister of War; and Jemal Pasha, Minister of Marine and later Military Governor of Syria. Of these more anon.

Each of the large areas in Turkey, such as Mesopotamia, or Syria, was divided into smaller sections called *vilāyets* under control of a Governor-General, or *Vāli*,[1] who was responsible only to the Sultan; or in other words, to the control of the Committee of Union and Progress. During the military régime in Syria the *Vālis* were limited in their functions by the power of the Military Governor. The *vilāyet* contained four graded subdivisions the officials of which were all responsible to the *Vāli*. The *vilāyet* boundaries for the most part followed some logical geographic divisions. However, Beirût *Vilāyet*, in which we lived, contained three separate areas around Beirût, Sidon and Tripoli, where the Province of Lebanon extended to the seacoast and cut into it in two places, and a fourth part comprising Nâblus in Palestine. The *Vilāyet* of Beirût which included so many detached sections is only one of a dozen illustrations of how Syria was through her government and through her very nature internally disintegrated.

One of the chief causes of this disintegration was the physical character of Syria. There are two practically parallel ranges of mountains extending through almost its entire length. The first, or Western Range, is near the coast, with which it is connected by a chain of coastal plains of greatly varied widths. The second, or Eastern Range, is on the side toward the Syrian Desert. Between these is a narrow depression, or rift, which is, at the Dead Sea, the lowest level on the face of the earth. Thus at almost any point where you cross Syria going eastward you find five parallel

[1] Turkish—*Vilāyet* and *Vāli*; Arabic—*Wilâyeh* and *Wâli*.

bands: coastal plain, mountain, rift, mountain, desert.

The diversity of surface in Syria produces an equal diversity in climate, and this diversity is paralleled by the variety of races and religions. The bulk of the population of Syria is Arab in origin, and is of two general classes, the settled, or Felahin, and the nomadic, or Bedouin.

The settled population is of very mixed blood. It includes the Syrians, by which we mean the descendants of all those peoples, except the Jews, who spoke Aramaic at the beginning of the Christian era. This stock is modified by an admixture of Arab and Crusader blood, and its language is now Arabic. The Syrians present a great diversity of types. There are the half-nomad, crude farmer folk of the borderland between civilization and the desert, the more advanced farmer class of the mountain districts, the conservative inhabitants of the inland cities, and the fairly cosmopolitan people of the coast cities. Scattered through nearly all these classes is a gradually increasing leaven of education.

Besides the divisions created by location and by occupation there are still others created by religion. In America one asks, What is a man's profession? In Syria, What is his religion? Some of the Syrians became Moslems at the time of the Turkish conquests, but a very large proportion are still Christians. The latter are of many denominations, often with antagonistic interests. Probably the foremost bodies among them are the Greek Orthodox and the Maronites, the latter adherents of a modified form of the Roman Catholic Church. The Maronites have long been sympathetic with French interests in Syria; and together with the Druzes, their rivals, are destined to play, in the immediate future, a prominent part in the life of their country.

The Druzes are a mixed race, mostly of Arab blood. They possess a secret religion which may be termed a mixture of Islâm and Christianity in a more or less esoteric form. They also believe in a series of incarnations of the soul after death until its final absorption into the Deity. The Druzes formerly lived in feudal state under Sheikhs, who were in turn subject to Emirs. They rose to power in the early part of the sixteenth century, and maintained their supremacy until 1860. Numerically they are still the strongest of the non-Christian sects in Lebanon, and they cherish a deep-rooted hatred of the Christians which finds frequent vent in local feuds. Practically all the Moslems in Lebanon are heretical, and are probably as antagonistic toward the orthodox adherents of Islâm as they are toward the Christians. While the Druzes are the most numerous of the schismatic sects, there are a number of others, notably the Mutawailehs, and the Nusairiyeh.

This bird's-eye view of the principal racial and religious divisions in Syria shows how lacking the country is in national unity. When, owing to the exigencies of war, internal communications were reduced to the minimum, or in some parts entirely suspended, the physical and racial characteristics of Syria were such that parts of the country became as much cut off as oases in the desert which caravans rarely touch. Hence, while Syria is not large, we in Beirût were practically out of contact with certain regions comparatively near us. Other sections, however, claiming attention for their very isolation, had in a marked degree a bearing on the internal situation of the country during the war.

Most travellers approaching Syria by sea usually notice first the character of its coast; for if the sea be rough, they may not be able to land. The coast is regular and possesses no good harbours, even Beirût with a port in the sheltering curve of St. George's Bay offers but fickle entrance in bad weather. The striking feature of the Syrian seaboard along half its length is the mountains which seem to rise abruptly from the sea.

There are, however, about eight maritime plains whose location is indicated on the map by the larger rivers or by the more important seaboard towns which have naturally developed near them. A narrow strip, in some places scarce wide enough for a roadway, connects these plains. The close proximity of the mountains on one side and of the sea on the other makes the scenery varied and lovely. Now and again the level areas expand into tracts of great fertility whose abundant yield of fruit, vegetables, and other crops supplies the needs of the coast cities and provides them with produce for export. Except in two large plains south of Mt. Carmel there is little grain raised near the sea, which explains why the coast of Syria north of Palestine is dependent on the interior for its main staple, wheat.

On leaving the coast and entering the mountains one finds another distinct area, the Lebanon district. It derives its name from the Lebanon Mountains—sometimes erroneously spoken of as Mount Lebanon—a mighty range which begins northeast of Tripoli and extends approximately to a region east of Sidon and Tyre. The Lebanon Mountains contain the highest peaks of the Western Range in a ridge called Dahr-el-Ḳodib, southeast of Tripoli. The rugged nature of the country with its high mountains and steep-sided valleys has produced a hardy, energetic race of mountaineers, physically vigorous, honest and free-spirited.

The antagonism between the Druzes and the Maronites early resulted in lack of cohesion in the Lebanon, and foreign intrigue and Turkish hatred of all Christian subjects played upon the religious feud. The Moslem Government first covertly incited the Druzes against the Christians, and then openly abetted them. As a result of this plotting, the Lebanon Mountains became in 1860 the scene of a tragedy so horrible that the Foreign Powers realized the necessity for prompt and effective intervention. In this year occurred the massacre of the Christians by the Druzes in some scores of Lebanon villages and the slaughter of about three thousand Christians in Damascus. During that reign of terror the foreign residents underwent a most anxious time. In view of the fact that the Ottoman Government would do nothing to restore order, the European Powers found it necessary to intervene in

Lebanon, which was occupied by 20,000 foreign troops, about half of which were French.

The French occupation continued till 1861 when the Sublime Porte was forced to accede to an arrangement which would tend to lessen quarrels between the Christians and the Druzes. Even after the withdrawal of foreign troops, French and English naval squadrons cruised along the coast for months,. just as they did from 1915 to 1918 for other reasons. Lebanon was constituted a Privileged Province by statute of September 6, 1864, with an autonomous government under the protection of the five Great Powers: England, France, Italy, Austria, and Germany. The Governor of Lebanon was to be a Christian, a just precaution considering the fact that three-fourths of the population were Christians, and arrangements were made for the gradual withdrawal of the Druzes from the jurisdiction of the State.

In 1914, when the Ottoman Empire broke relations with the Entente Powers, Lebanon ceased to be regarded as an Independent Protectorate. It was ranked as an Independent *Mutaṣerrifiyeh* and given a Moslem Governor, or *Mutaṣerrif*, responsible to the Sultan. Curiously enough, while the Turk violated during the Great War every other treaty he had ever signed, for some unknown reason he respected the exemption of the Lebanese from military service. Up to within the last few years Lebanon had her own army of only a few hundred men, and no Lebanese could be drafted for service in the Turkish army. The Lebanese uniform was not unlike the Zouave, and it was so novel a sight as to impress the traveller as almost an anachronism to see these husky mountaineers in their blue and red uniforms, with little bolero jackets and full, baggy trousers, standing guard along the roads, or sauntering about the stations as the trains pulled in.

It was always with a sense of relief that one crossed the *vilāyet* boundary and passed into the region guarded by these Lebanese. The Lebanon roads were always in better condition than those which the *vilāyet* was supposed to care for, and the very people seemed of a finer type as soon as one entered Lebanon. During the war they were so fortunate as to have Turkish governors that were reasonable and conscientious. Ali Munif Bey, later Minister of Public Works, and Ismail Hakki, former Turkish Counsellor in Egypt, both tried to deal as fairly by their province as the Turkish Government and certain unavoidable circumstances would permit. Yet Lebanon suffered more heavily during the years of the war than any other part of Syria. Practically three-fourths of her population of approximately half a million were wiped out by starvation.

The reason for this was that the rugged Lebanon district, unfit for much level cultivation, raised only a small fraction of the wheat necessary for her population. For their income the Lebanese depended on the sale of produce from their small farms or the export of their silk. Also certain villages were supported by special trades; for instance, one depended on silver filagree work, another on knife-making, while a third made nearly all the bells which called Christians to worship from Aintab to Sinai. The Entente blockade, instituted the second year of the war, caused the cessation of numerous small industries such as those just mentioned and the temporary destruction of the silk-raising industry, inasmuch as all the silk could not be marketed in the country, but was usually exported to France. Later, under the guise of military necessity, Jemal Pasha confiscated all the silk that he could lay his hands on, and he used as his agent a notorious rascal, Tewfik Bey. The poor suffered most heavily, as the rich were able to give large enough bribes to secure protection. Still another cause of distress was the fact that, owing to the complete cessation of postal communication with the outside world, a large number of Lebanese were deprived of external sources of income, such as funds sent them by relatives resident in America or in other countries, or bank accounts which they had established abroad. It so happened, therefore, that for one reason or another whole villages were annihilated.

The Government commandeered wholesale, without payment, animals for transport and for army food supply. People dependent on their sheep or mules for support were impoverished, and there were no longer enough animals for the transport of foodstuffs from one place to another, a serious matter in view of the fact that the railways, being in Turkish or German hands, were available only for military use. Farmers who had saved seed-wheat the first year of the war were forced to eat it the second summer, and by the second winter Lebanon was bereft of wheat. Her discouraged, almost hopeless population found their country isolated by reason of its rugged mountains and the desire of the Turkish Government to cut it off from the rest of Syria.

Had the Turk permitted it, the whole of Syria might have been fed by the two main inland areas, the vast level tracts in the Central Depression and the Ḥaurân. Around Aleppo, Ḥamâ, and Ḥoms the apparently bare and uninteresting levels are capable of raising a great deal of wheat. These plains during the war were entirely separated from each other and from the rest of Syria, save for roads over mountain passes or the slender thread of the railway between Aleppo and Reyâk, the only means by which, after endless difficulties in the matter of purchase, permits, and car-space, anything could be transported from this region to other parts of Syria.

Still more isolated was Ḥaurân, the great wheat-raising region of Syria, which once fed half the Roman world. The plateau of Ḥaurân lies south of Damascus and adjacent to it is another wheat country, Jebel ed-Druz, or Druze Mountain. The inhabitants of this part of Syria are partly settled Bedouin tribes and partly, as the name indicates, Druzes. They have always retained distinctive tribal characteristics and customs, and have maintained an exclusive and often hostile attitude, at times quite baffling to the Turk. When the Government essayed to control the vast supplies of wheat raised in Ḥaurân the population made endless difficulties and even concealed quantities of the grain. They also refused Turkish paper money, and

would sell only to buyers who could offer gold " with
the horse on it," *i. e.*, English sovereigns bearing the
mounted St. George combating the dragon.

Because food was the crying need of all Syria during
the war, these parts of the country I have mentioned
somewhat at length were constantly in the minds of all
of us. The coast, dependent both on external and internal trade relations, was isolated on both sides and
suffering; Lebanon was segregated, internally dis-
rupted and starving; the two sections of the interior
which might have been utilized to feed the rest of the
country were forced into passivity by the Turks.
Moreover, not only did the native population suffer at
the hands of their rulers, but there was scattered all
over Syria the large non-Syrian element mentioned
earlier in this book, the Armenians, Jews, Levantines
and foreign residents, whose fortunes were bound up
in the fate of the country, and whose sufferings were
similar to those of the Syrians.

Not only did each separate community struggle for
existence, but Syria as a whole was a victim because
her position geographically and politically facilitated
her becoming a closed highway. Her inhabitants suffered because physically, racially and politically Syria
was isolated and lacked cohesion. The Americans
resident in the country felt it their task to do what they
could to alleviate internal conditions. It is to Turkey,
however, and to her ally, Germany, that Syria owes the
fact of her remaining for nearly five years behind a
drawn curtain.

III

FOREIGN GUESTS OF THE SULTAN IN SYRIA

MY first introduction to Syria was through the letters of my aunt who lived there, and I was perplexed to account for the fact that these letters bore the postage-stamps of any one of five different nations. The geographies said that Syria was a Turkish province, but what could be the status of a country whose postal service was apparently under international control? Later, when I myself went to live with that aunt in Syria, I learned that the answer lay in that half-mysterious phrase, " the Capitulations,"—what the Capitulations were and how they affected Turkey will later be discussed in detail. The question of the political status of Syria arises in the mind of each new arrival in the land. A more composite population could hardly be imagined, and unlike most places where the population is international, in Syria the subjects of each foreign nation maintain to an extraordinary degree the integrity of their national life.

In Crusading days, all Europeans were grouped by their Eastern opponents under the title of *Frank*, and to-day a corruption of the term still exists in the

Syrian word *Franji*. The Syrians themselves have drawn this line of demarkation, designating as *Franji* any Occidental, European or American, and with them the word is practically synonymous with foreigner. It might seem that the result would be a social homogeneity among the Westerners resident in Syria, but such is not the case. It is true to a certain extent in the smaller places; but in large cities, like Beirût, the foreign population as a whole has never amalgamated. One finds oneself speaking of " the French colony," or the " Anglo-American community," and each one of these units is socially self-sufficient. True, there are frequent occasions when all forgather, and the assembly takes on a truly cosmopolitan character, but in general, in the ordinary world of social life, each colony lives very much unto itself.

The East has always been attractive for the Western world. Its lure has wooed men from home and kindred to endure danger and hardships in a hostile land, and this siren call is as compelling to many of us to-day as it was to our ancestors centuries ago. Long before the fire of religious enthusiasm roused in Europe the determination to gain possession of the shrines of the Holy Land, trade between the Occident and the Orient had existed to their mutual profit. In the beginning, the current was from the East westward, for civilization matured more rapidly in the warm Eastern climes. The Phœnicians who, centuries before the Christian Era, were masters of the Syrian coast, built their ships and ventured forth, even beyond the Pillars of Hercules, into the boundless ocean of the

West. They bore their treasures to that little isle which we now call England, and brought back with them ores and furs which they had there obtained in fair exchange. Rome turned her eyes toward the East, and seeing that it was good, overthrew great kingdoms and annexed vast tracts of territory. Even among the Crusaders, political and commercial interests were paramount over their enthusiasm for the holy cause. Especially was this true of the Fourth Crusade (1204 A. D.), which Venice actually diverted from the Holy Land to Dalmatia and Constantinople for purposes of her own trade and by secret agreement with her Eastern commercial allies.

The vast armies of Crusaders, recruited from all the countries of Europe, and comprising men of all walks of life, were moved by varied and often conflicting interests. Shoulder to shoulder with the religious fanatic marched the social outcast who sought to obliterate the memory of his past offences against society by the fame of his prowess in a holy cause. Their tent-mates were an adventurer, restless and chafed under the humdrum conditions of every-day life, and a prosperous merchant who thought in terms of commercial profit.

The same impulses which prompted men of wholly diverse tastes to join in the Crusades have brought the modern Westerners to the Holy Land. Some are actuated by the pure spirit of missionary zeal and religious fervour, others by the no less altruistic desire to encourage the advance of these less progressive countries through commerce, agriculture, and the development of natural resources. Still others are inspired solely by selfish motives, and by recognition of the fact that in a country which has so obvious a future as Syria it is well to be first on the scene. According as their motives have been laudable or deplorable, the influence of foreigners on the country has been beneficial or unfortunate. From the very dawn of her history, Syria has been the bone of contention and the prey of conflicting desires. She has been the victim of religious fanaticism no less than the object of crass commercialism. She has been riven with civil dissension, and has been rent in the conflict of international jealousies. And yet, for the present, her salvation lies in the beneficent and just intervention of some great power, under whose mandate she may learn to master her own forces, and develop her independence.

Among the alien races which have exploited Syria none have wrought such ravages as the Turks. The recent history of the country has been one long succession of conflicts between Christianity and Islâm, and each power in turn has worsted the other and assumed governmental control. During the twelfth and thirteenth centuries in particular, the struggles between the two religions were titanic, and Christian kings and Moslem princes succeeded each other with melodramatic rapidity. The later Crusades were fruitless, and after the failure in 1248 of the Thirteenth and last Crusade, Islâm for nearly seven centuries was never effectively disputed. Indeed, until the nineteenth century, foreign Christians were barely tolerated in the Holy Land, and it is only during the last century that they have gained an effective foothold there. Very quietly and unostentatiously Christian influence has spread until, with the British occupation in 1918, Syria once more passed into Christian hands. So complete, however, has been the transformation, that the population is no longer overwhelmingly Moslem, although the Moslems in all localities but Lebanon are still in the majority. The Crusade of the last few centuries has been a silent one, but the West has made its contribution of men and resources just as truly as it did in the days of chivalry. The saint, the merchant, the outlaw, the adventurer are still to be found among these modern crusaders, and all the races of the Occident are represented in that army.

From the point of view of numbers, the influence of the Anglo-Americans is probably greatest in Syria, and as the aims and ideals of these two nations are not dissimilar, it is fair, up to a certain point, to treat the two as one for purposes of discussion. Previous to the war, there were several hundred British and Americans resident in Syria, the majority of whom were engaged in missionary and educational work. From Jerusalem to Aleppo, from the seacoast to the wilderness east of the Jordan, in the mountains, in the desert, and on the fertile maritime plain scores of mission stations were scattered In an important city like Beirût, there might be a dozen missions operating simultaneously and harmoniously, carrying on evangelistic, educational, medical, and social work. In more isolated spots one foreign pastor was located, or one British or American doctor ministering to the needs of the district by his efforts as a touring physician, or by the maintenance of an up-to-date hospital. In still other centers, according to their size, a school or groups of schools were located.

This organized mission-work had been gradually developing in the country during the last hundred years. In the early years of the nineteenth century, the first American missionaries penetrated into Syria, and began their work on the same far-reaching scale which the present century has elaborated and developed, but has not radically changed. The first British mission in the Holy Land was established about the same time, and so rapidly did the work grow that at the opening of the war there was hardly an important city in Syria or Palestine, or even, one might say, a central village that was not a base for missionary operations.

The main centers of missionary activity were, naturally, the largest cities, such as Beirût, Damascus, Aleppo, Jerusalem, Jaffa, Ḥaifâ, Sidon and Tripoli. Other towns were occupied, however, according to the opportunities that they offered for contact with an important social community. In a little, out-of-the-way town in Northern Galilee, for instance, there is an independent mission-worker who has been prompted to devote her life to the conversion of Jews; and who has chosen this particular village as the best means of access to a large Jewish district. To Nebk and Deir 'Aṭîyeh, remote villages on the skirts of the Syrian desert, a small band of Danish missionaries has penetrated, largely because this region has been left untouched by other missionary organizations. Certain

villages in Lebanon have been chosen because they are
the strongholds of the Druzes, others because they
offer access to some of the more inquiring sects of Oriental Christians who have begun to evince an interest
in the Western Church. In this way the whole country has been fairly honeycombed with Anglo-American
influence; and it speaks well for the spirit in which the
foreigners have laboured, that, wherever he may be,
the missionary is almost an oracle in his community.
Perhaps the strongest impetus the Syrian nation has
had toward national unity has come from this common
admiration for individuals living among them, who are
not of them.

Much of this incipient welding of sects and races
that have been traditionally antagonistic must surely be
credited to various missionary enterprises in the country. The Syrian Protestant College, formerly the child
of the American Congregational Mission in Syria, but
now under independent management, has been one of
the most prominent factors in producing this spirit of
tolerance. It is a recognized fact that the Moslem,
the Jew, the Druze, the Protestant, and the Oriental
Christian who have been students in this College can
work together as business men, or can serve on the
same committee, with a degree of success that would
be absolutely impossible had they not had this levelling
experience of a tolerant American education. The
same is true to a lesser degree of the graduates of the
American mission-schools, and this only because the
pupils are less mature, and their characters less stabil-
ized when they leave the secondary schools. When

they graduate from the College they are men, and their opinions are formulated with more or less permanency. The graduate of the American High School is still a callow youth, and unless he continue under the influence of mature minds in some more advanced school, he may surrender himself anew to the intolerant prejudices of his own sect.

Among the foreign organizations in Syria and Palestine the French missions come next to the British and American in scope and influence. It is an open secret, however, that while the latter are operating in the country from purely humanitarian motives, French missions have been established with a more subtle political purpose. It has, moreover, been unfortunate for their influence in the country that a large number of the French priests who have emigrated to Syria were ejected from France, where they were considered undesirable citizens. This has not, however, prevented their being used by their Government as agents of political propaganda, and they have gained a following of several hundred thousand among the Maronites, the most powerful sect of Syrian Romanists.

The particular stronghold of the French missions is the Lebanon, and there is hardly a hillcrest that is not crowned with a Catholic monastery; there is scarcely a spot in Lebanon so remote that in the evening hush one cannot hear the melodious note of a convent-bell sounding the hour of evening worship. The terms Catholic and Maronite and French-sympathizer are practically synonymous in Syria, for most of the Syrians who acknowledge the authority of the Pope look also to

France as their strongest hope in the attainment of their political aspirations. Undoubtedly the French have done a great deal for the country in the matter of education, but it has been unfortunate that this has been accomplished at the price of exaggerating the already latent denominational antagonisms. Their most distinguished institution in Syria is the Jesuit University in Beirût, which has won international recognition for the high standard of its scholarship, its famous library, and the value of some of its publications, especially along historical and archæological lines.

Among the Protestant missions operating in Syria and Palestine before the war were the Danish, previously mentioned, and the German. Curiously enough, the latter were assigned by their government no rôle as political agents, in spite of Germany's long-acknowledged political aspirations in Syria. In Beirût and in Jerusalem in particular there were numerous flourishing institutions, hospitals, hospices, orphanages and schools; but at the time of writing these are all under the control of British or American organizations. There were three prosperous German colonies in Palestine, one at Jerusalem, chiefly commercial, one at Jaffa, and one at Ḥaifâ, the two latter mainly agricultural. These colonies were established about fifty years ago by modern crusaders from Würtemburg who were inspired with the desire to rebuild the Temple. Since the British occupation, the Germans, with but few exceptions, have been expelled from the territory of the former Turkish Empire; and it has not yet been decided whether they will be permitted to return.

This brief statement of foreign missionary influence in Syria would not be complete without reference to the work of numerous other nationalities; but as most of their activity has been along the line of Catholic missionary methods—the domination of the few, rather than the lifting of the masses—their influence has been restricted and purely local. The Russians had extensive work, especially in Palestine, where, previous to the war, the richly endowed Russian Palestine Society maintained numerous hospices and schools, including a normal seminary. The Russians have always particularly patronized the adherents of the Greek Orthodox Church in Syria, all of whom were admittedly Russian in sympathy.

The Austrians and Italians likewise supported missions in the Holy Land, but their work was preëminently educational, or medical, and was not extensive in scope. Among the foreigners must also be included the " Frank " monks, who have long possessed monasteries in the Holy Land. The Franciscans have been especially zealous in providing accommodations at many different places for wayfaring pilgrims. These monks are generally Spanish, or Italian, and more rarely French. They exercise a very beneficial influence over the native clergy through the schools which they maintain.

As was intimated, however, at the beginning of this chapter, secular interests as well as religious motives have attracted the Westerner to the Near East. There has always been a rich field for commercial enterprise, and previous to the war European finance had been granted important concessions in Syria. There was a complete system of German banks throughout every part of the Turkish Empire, but only one other foreign bank existed in Syria, a French bank in Jerusalem. All the leading European nations, except Germany, however, had contributed liberally to the currency supply of Turkey, with a result that French, Italian, Russian and British gold were as much in circulation as was Turkish gold.

The French in particular had extensive commercial interests, and consequently definite political aspirations. Such vital factors in the life of the country as the railways, roads, tramlines, and the gas and electric companies were backed by foreign capital. A French company had built the seawall at Beirût and controlled the port. The same was true of the Damascus, Hedjaz and Extension Railroad, and of the Gas and Electric Company of Beirût. The concession for the Bagdad Railway, on the other hand, had been granted to Germany, although at one time England had been almost in sight of the prize. The Beirût Tram Company was a Belgian concern: all of which indicates how keenly desirable a foothold in this little land was adjudged by the great European Powers. Ships of all nations brought foreign produce to the Syrian coast; and, incidentally, America made her contribution to the economy of Turkey by the importation of the Standard Oil Company's products, and by the exportation of tobacco and licorice. An American-Syrian Chamber of Commerce was in existence before the war, and is now being revived; but in comparison with other foreign countries America's interests were so limited to educational and religious enterprises as to seem to the Turks of little consequence. They realized that America had no desire to interfere in the politics of the Near East, and this fact gave her a prestige wholly different from that of any other Great Power. During practically the whole course of the war the Ottoman attitude toward the United States was conciliatory and ingratiating; and even the Germans failed to blind the Turks to the fact that, if they alienated America, they would lose their one possible champion. In view of the fact that, at the opening of the war, America was generally supposed to be destined for the rôle of international arbiter at the final settlement of peace, Turkey stubbornly persisted in maintaining amiable relations with this desirable friend.

One has only to recall the history of the Turkish Empire to realize how absolutely essential it was, if foreigners were to reside there at all, that their life and property should be protected by special treaties and agreements. Such treaties have existed for centuries, and are known as "the Capitulations." I have here taken the liberty of quoting a few admirably concise paragraphs from *Ambassador Morgenthau's Story* on this subject:

"Turkey had never been admitted to a complete equality with European nations, and in reality she had never been an independent sovereignty. The Sultan's laws and customs differed so radically from those of Europe and America that no non-Moslem country could think of submitting its citizens in Turkey to them. In many matters, therefore, the principle of exterritoriality had always prevailed in favour of all citizens or subjects of countries enjoying capitulatory rights. Almost all European countries, as well as the United States, for centuries had had their own consular courts and prisons in which they tried and punished crimes which their nationals committed in Turkey. We all had our schools, which were subject, not to Turkish law and protection, but to that of the country which maintained them. Several nations had their own post offices, as they did not care to submit their mail to the Ottoman postal service. Turkey likewise did not have unlimited power of taxation over foreigners. It could not even increase their customs taxes without the consent of the foreign Powers. . . . Turkey was thus prohibited by the Powers from developing any industries of her own; instead, she was forced to take large quantities of inferior articles from Europe. Against these restrictions Turkish statesmen had protested for years, declaring that they constituted an insult to their pride as a nation and also interfered with their progress." [1]

Only under these provisions, as experience subsequent to their abolition certainly proved, could life for the foreign resident in Turkey maintain any degree of safety or security. By grace of these treaties, he was not only permitted to pursue his work unmolested, but he had the right of appeal to his national representatives at the Sublime Porte in case of any infringement of his treaty rights. It may easily be understood that

[1] *Ambassador Morgenthau's Story*, pp. 112–113.

these Capitulations were a thorn in the flesh of the Turk, or one might better say, a ring in the nose of the bull.   If ever he so far forgot himself as to menace his foreign guests, a judicious twist would recall him to his actual position, and frighten him into at least a pretence of submission.   However, he was biding his time, and it will shortly be seen that the first acts of independence and defiance committed by the Turk, under the instigation of the Germans, were the abolition of the Capitulations and the celebration of this event with public demonstrations and rejoicing.

IV

MOBILIZING AN ELUSIVE ARMY

THE curtain rises on Syria. Time: the summer of 1914. The heat in Beirût during June and July had been most oppressive, and long before the beginning of August most of the American community had fled from the torrid humidity of the plain to their summer-homes in the mist-swept retreats of Lebanon. Only the President of the Syrian Protestant College, the Staff of the College Hospitals, and the Manager of the American Press were detained in the city by the pressure of their duties, which were, if anything, heavier during the summer months, when illness was more prevalent, or plans must be made for the work of the coming winter season. But even these busy folk found it necessary to seek refreshment in the hills, and counted it among their duties to arrange an occasional holiday in Lebanon. On Saturday, August first, Mr. and Mrs. Dana and I set out for the village of Shweir where we expected to pass a quiet and peaceful week-end. As a matter of fact, I recall a restful and idle Sunday spent under the pines on the mountainside. However, the memory of that uneventful day has been almost obliterated by the excitement of the events that followed. On Monday morning we were returning to the heat and dust of the plain and the work of another trying week when we met crowds of people fleeing from the city. Every one seemed panic-stricken, and many urged us to retrace our steps to the mountains. In vain we attempted to discover the cause of this feverish excitement. It was evident that no great catastrophe had befallen the city, for there it lay on the plain beneath us, pale and drowsy in the August heat. Not a wisp of smoke was visible to give the alarm of fire, nothing appeared out of the ordinary to stir the slumbering countryside, except the unusual clouds of dust raised by the hurrying feet of men and animals toiling up the steep ascent. At times we almost feared that we too should have to join that witless exodus, for on several occasions we were stopped by travellers and told that if we attempted to cross the borderline between Lebanon and Beirût *Vilâyet* our horses would be commandeered by the military. As a matter of fact, we only succeeded in reaching our destination in the heart of the city because we insisted on our right as Americans to pursue our journey unmolested, an argument which continued effective until the war was several months old. When we reached the city and reliable sources of information, we discovered the cause of the panic. The Austrian guns had opened fire on Belgrade, and with the echo of the first report the Turkish Government had begun to mobilize its army. It was from the traditional horrors of enforced service in the Turkish ranks that the Syrians were fleeing as one man.

There was nothing of Oriental sluggishness in the

way that Turkey acted in this crisis, and we in the country were wholly swept off our feet. We hardly realized even at that time how powerful the German influence in the Empire already was, for it had been fostered so secretly, and yet so skillfully, that when the crisis came, Germany alone had her hand on the rudder. When the shot was fired at Sarajevo, Germany warned Turkey to prepare herself against the attack which must surely follow the outbreak of trouble in the Balkans, and at the drop of the hat Turkey was in the ring. In every country of Europe nations were beginning to stir, men were donning uniforms, and the most peaceful land was being converted into an enormous drill-ground. Turkey in this respect was no exception, but where the men of other nations responded willingly to the call of their country, in Turkey they fled before the conscription officers as from the plague. Even the Lebanese dared not rely on their traditional immunity from military service as long as they resided in Beirût, for no one trusted the wily Turk, and each felt that he would be safe only in the fastnesses of Lebanon among his compatriots who could combine with him to defend their rights. It would hardly be incorrect to say that there was not an Ottoman subject in all of Syria who was animated by one spark of patriotism. Of the Syrians themselves, a great majority secretly aspired to independence, or to a protectorate under the mandate of one of the Great Powers. Others, less nationalistically ambitious and concerned solely with their own personal well-being, were planning to leave their native land and seek their fortunes abroad where, under a more beneficent administration, they might live in peace and devote themselves to the acquisition of wealth. To such the war was a calamity only because it trapped them in Syria when they were intending to fare forth into the world overseas. Even the Turkish government officials had no love for Turkey, and felt no responsibility to their government. Greed and the accumulation of wealth were their sole aims in life, and to them the war offered a possibility of greater license than had prevailed in times of peace.

Then it was that Turkey, hounded on one side by Germany, was driven on the other side by a nascent hope that, by the proper conduct of her affairs at this time, when the world was in a tumult and every one was too much occupied with his own affairs to concern himself with the Near-Eastern question, she might pay off old scores, and secure to herself certain much-coveted privileges, and, perchance, even additional territory. If she listened to German warnings, she became convinced that her very national existence was at stake, and that only by the instant mobilization of her armies and prompt resort to precautionary measures against foreigners could she hope to maintain her separate identity. If she lent an ear to the voice of her own avarice, she saw in the world-calamity an occasion to establish beyond question her disputed sway over Egypt, and to drive the hated and privileged foreigners from her territory. Whichever motive actuated her conduct, certain it was that she must have an army, and the only way to mobilize that army was by force.

To assemble that army, however, was like trying to gather feathers in a gale. The only hope lay in immediate action. If she loosed her hand from one captured feather to seize another, a puff of wind carried the first far out of reach. The available men of the country were scurrying to Lebanon like rabbits making for cover, and those who were obliged to remain within the *vilāyet* were daily disappearing from view. No one knew whither they had gone, or how they lived, but many who had been familiar sights in the genial haunts of the city vanished overnight, and were not seen again for months—in some cases even for the whole period of the war. Where they hid themselves we are only now beginning to learn, but with the desperation of the outlaw they fled from the conscription officers of the Government.

Certain features of the resulting chaos in Syria need not be described, for there was not a country of Europe that did not know the same upheaval during some period of the war. But the abject terror that possessed the population as a mass is something that has probably never been equalled in this generation. Belgium was undoubtedly terrorized when the wave of German invasion broke over her boundaries, but the necessity for immediate action for self-defence, and the purifying love of country transformed that terror into a sacred fervour. In Turkey, on the other hand, there was no redeeming virtue to ennoble this consuming fear. It was the repellent fright of the animal at bay that swept over the land from one end to the other. All sects were united in the common bond of fear of the Government and in the search for some escape from the certain disaster which loomed ahead.

Even the most pessimistic did not imagine in those days that the war would last more than two or three months at most, or that the conflagration once kindled would lick up everything in its path. No one really believed that any of Turkey's enemies would take this occasion for attacking her; otherwise perhaps the age-long hatred of one Balkan nation for another, or the traditional enmity between Russia and Turkey, might have united the peoples of the Ottoman Empire in a common cause. The threat that England would send an army from Egypt to invade Palestine, or that France would disembark her legions on the maritime plain failed to arouse any military fervour in the heart of the Syrian who was secretly hoping, even plotting, that England or France might come and deliver the country from the hand of the oppressor. We all believed in those days that one or both of those Powers would undoubtedly attack Turkey should the latter show the supreme folly of allying herself with Germany in the war, but that Turkey would ever be capable of such madness we hardly imagined.

One who had been absent from Syria between Saturday, August first, and Monday, August tenth, might have fancied that he had suffered the fate of Rip Van Winkle, and that in reality some years had elapsed in the interval. In those ten days the whole country had been transformed. Where, before that Saturday, men had gone quietly about their business, cultivating their ground, carrying on their commercial and financial transactions as they had been wont during times of peace; on the Monday there were no young men to be seen in the streets, shops were closed, business was paralyzed, and the anxious countenances of women and children already bespoke fear and anxiety as to where they should find their next meal. Banks had closed their doors, the *moratorium* was in force, gold had gone into hiding, and those who had cash in hand when the bolt struck were hoarding it against the needs of the unknown future. The low capitalization of the country necessarily forces the people to a hand-to-mouth existence. Even a man who owns much land has so little ready money that he cannot afford to lay in extensive quantities of living commodities, but must depend upon daily cash-purchases in the markets. Within a fortnight the necessity of acquiring ready cash had brought into the market many valuable personal effects such as rugs and jewelry. No one would sell for credit, and the would-be purchaser must lay down the cold coin, even though he had to sell his watch to secure it.

The result in the cities was the suspension of all industries. Factories were closed, and petty merchants reduced their business to a minimum. In the country it was harvest time when many of the men were taken for the army, and there was no one left to garner the crops. Thousands of dollars' worth of foodstuffs rotted in the fields, and when the winter came with its icy rains and penetrating winds, thousands starved for want of the precious, wasted food. It was not only the habitually indigent, or even the labourers who led a hand-to-mouth existence, that began to feel the pinch of poverty. All classes, with but one exception, were stricken with want; and some of those who had lived in luxury before the war, because of their inability to realize ready cash on their invested capital, knew now the pangs of hunger.

With the rupture of diplomatic relations between Turkey and the Entente, the British, French, and Russian steamers discontinued their service to Turkish ports. All possibilities of import were thus cut off. Certain staples of diet, such as sugar, which are not raised anywhere within the Empire, could no longer be brought into the country, and the same was true of less necessary articles, such as drugs, matches, Russian oil, and foreign clothing. Duty on some imports was raised one hundred per cent., and in a few weeks the Beirût Customs-House was closed, although it contained over one million dollars' worth of goods which the owners could not afford to clear.

Within a very short time the general supply of stores in the country was exhausted, or had been hidden, especially in those places where soldiers had been stationed and where the shops had been looted on the pretext of supplying the needs of the army. An inventory of the articles commandeered, including not only clothing and food, but babies' slippers, silk petticoats, and face-powder, will reveal how wholesale and shameless was the robbery. No receipts were given, and no payments were made for anything taken. The whole proceeding was equivalent to mob-plunder carried on by soldiers or by government representatives. Then, when it seemed that everything seizable had been seized, there came a new order that every shopkeeper must furnish a statement of stores in his possession. He was indeed between the Devil and the deep sea. If he did not make a truthful declaration, he exposed himself to the penalty of fine and imprisonment; if he were honest, his little all would be taken.[1]

It would be impossible to imagine a more desperate situation. The economy of the country has already been dealt with in a previous chapter, and special emphasis was there laid on the fact that many thousands in Syria are wholly dependent for their support upon relatives resident abroad. Frequently the inhabitants of towns with a population of from three hundred to two thousand are almost entirely supported by relatives in the United States, South America, or the British Empire. Of late years this fact has changed the very aspect of the landscape. Wherever a neat red tile roof has replaced the old-fashioned flat mud roof on a house in a Syrian village, one may safely assume that the new roof has been purchased with the earnings of some Syrian who has prospered abroad. With Turkey's entrance into the war this income from the outside world was completely arrested. Checks and drafts were no longer negotiable, even when offered at a discount of fifty per cent. The difficulties of this situation which began in August were augmented still further by the declaration of hostilities between Turkey and the Entente in November, because of the fact

---

[1] *Vide* p. 6; also my *Report of the Beirût Red Cross Chapter,* May, 1915.

that ninety-nine per cent. of these remittances were by checks on London banking-houses, and the Turkish Government then decreed the transfer or negotiation of London drafts an illegal proceeding.

I have just said that all classes but one were levelled in the common distress and affliction that had befallen the country. That one exception was the class of wealthy merchants, those " wolfish " men, as some one recently described them, who had sufficient capital to enable them to speculate in foodstuffs, and who were so unprincipled as to feel no scruples against enriching themselves at the expense of their unfortunate country-men. With demoniacal foresight these capitalists real-ized their opportunity and bought up everything they could lay their hands on. By the time those who were less crafty in business affairs awoke to their extremely precarious situation and prepared to lay in a stock of necessary commodities, they discovered that the Syrian financiers had forestalled them. The whole reserve supply of the country was in the hands of speculators. All the sugar in a city like Beirût, which, if properly administered, should have supplied the wants of the entire population during practically the entire war, was stored in the warehouses of a wealthy Moslem, who preferred to let it rot, rather than put it on the market before he could command the price his avarice dictated. Early in the war most of the woolen and cotton goods of the country was bought up by wealthy Jews in Aleppo and dispatched to Bagdad, Constantinople, and other cities of the interior, leaving the markets of Syria absolutely stripped of anything which might be purchased, even at a ruinous price, for clothing or bedding. All the wheat in Syria was either commandeered by the military, or bought as it stood in the fields by these same crafty men of business; but when Lebanon lost thirty per cent. of her population through starvation in a single winter, the Government, which had connived at this robbery, pled difficulties of transport as an excuse for the fact that thousands of tons of wheat lay moulding in Damascus, Aleppo, and the Haurân. As a matter of fact, the whole problem of transport has been greatly exaggerated. It did not even require organization, and had the Government not interfered, the distribution of food supplies in the country might easily have been adjusted. The rich wheat regions of Haurân, Palestine and Northern Syria were fully capable of producing wheat sufficient for the needs of all Syria. One can easily understand that every car on the railway from Constantinople to Jerusalem carried troops and ammunition in one direction only, south, and that those same cars returned empty through the grain regions of Palestine and Haurân, where wheat sufficient to provide for the whole population of Syria lay piled on either side of the railway awaiting transport to distributing centers. The Government not only made no effort to regulate the revictualing of the country, but coöperated with the food-speculators who recognized in the economic situation the opportunity to amass enormous private fortunes. Permits for the purchase and transport of tremendous amounts of foodstuffs were granted to these speculators which less favoured merchants could not possibly obtain, and all the grain that was imported into Syria was consigned to a few wealthy men who formed a wheat-combine and who dictated their own exorbitant prices. Within a half-year after the commencement of the war in Europe a score of men in Syria held the country in the hollow of their hands. Commerce was at a complete standstill, and supplies were shifted from place to place, or marketed only as these men decreed.

As time went on conditions grew steadily worse, both in the towns and in the country. The same desperation that had driven the city-dweller to sell his rugs, his furniture, his jewels, even his house, had forced the rural population to mortgage every spare metre of land. Only recently there came to my attention a typical instance. It was the case of a man who with his two daughters lived in Beit Meri, a large village in the mountains some fifteen miles beyond Beirût. His two sons had emigrated to New Zealand; and as their business there had proved prosperous, they had undertaken the entire support of their father and their two sisters. Up to the time when communications were abruptly terminated by the war, remittances from the sons had arrived regularly. The father was an industrious and self-respecting farmer, but he lived, as did practically all of his class, a day-to-day existence. When the crash came, he had nothing set aside for such an emergency. He was soon forced to sell a small piece of land, but the price it brought was only sufficient to provide his family with bread for a few months. In time he was driven down to the city in search of some one who would advance him money on the pledge that his sons would pay off his debts at the close of the war. He discovered two business men, formerly from his village but now resident in the city, who were willing to loan him money; but the price demanded was a promissory note at fifty-five per cent. compound interest, and the agreement to repay in gold after the war! The sum of eighty Turkish Liras, or $240, which he received in paper three years ago is to-day due at the amount of £350, or $1,425! This is only one true instance out of thousands.

The reader may well wonder what had been the fate of the foreign resident in Syria during this difficult period. It must have impressed him that Turkey had taken the bit in her teeth, and that neither the curb of the Capitulations, nor the fear of foreign intervention had power to check her in her mad plunge to destruction. As a matter of fact, every country in Europe was desperately preoccupied with its own affairs, and only Germany, who had her own reasons for watching Turkey's every move, had time to consider how she had been affected by the world upheaval. An American who was on friendly terms with the Syrian mayor of the village where he had his summer-home furnished me with conclusive proof that months previous to August, 1914, Germany's plans for Turkey's part in the war that she was meditating were as fully matured as were her plans for Europe. In April, 1914, the *Mukhtar* of B——, a prominent town near Damascus, received from his Turkish superiors sealed instructions which he was to hold for further orders. He told his American friend about this sealed envelope and they speculated as to its meaning. On the first of August the mystery was solved, when the *Mukhtar* received an order to open the envelope and found therein an army conscription-list for his district and mobilization orders designed by the Germans in accordance with their own plans of campaign. Of course, the head of every village or community in Syria had received similar orders in April and August, and it was this foresight on the part of the Turco-German military party at Constantinople which explains why it was that by August 4, 1914, there was posted in every town in the interior of Syria a list of those inhabitants liable for military service. We could not at the time understand the dispatch with which these lists had been prepared. When war actually began, the wisdom of Germany's provisions became evident.

Germany, with practically the whole of the civilized world ranged against her, at least in sympathy, if not on the actual battlefield, had calculated that her one hope of salvation lay in the proper manipulation of Turkey as a pawn in the game. Turkey as Germany's ally would be invaluable in the execution of Teutonic projects against Russia, India, Egypt and the Balkans. Yet Turkey as a power could not be relied on to play her part unaided. Germany knew that the weaker Turkey was nationally, the easier it would be to intimidate her into playing the rôle that German strategy had assigned her. Turkey, racked with internal ailments, financially, socially and economically ruined, would be far less of a problem from the German standpoint than a Turkey that could stand on her own feet. Germany, therefore, who acknowledged no law but that of her own necessity, did everything within her power to weaken the country as a whole and to direct its control into the hands of a few chosen men to whom the German Ambassador at Constantinople might dictate the demands of the Kaiser.

In some respects, nothing that Germany did in Europe, disgraceful as her conduct there was, revealed the true depravity of her national standards as did her relations with Turkey. The world feels no sympathy with Turkey, and civilization rejoices to-day that the five-century old régime of crime and bloodshed has at last come to an end; but even Turkey's villainy does not excuse the part that Germany played, indeed, it only makes it worse. Can the world forgive a man with the education and traditions of a gentleman who hires an assassin to fight his battles with him, and who, worse still, does so without any intention of being loyal to the bond which he has himself established with his tool? Germany needed Turkey, but she meant to sell her when the proper time came.

In my opinion, however, Germany's supreme act of infamy was her attempt to incite the Moslem world to the *Jehâd*, or Sacred War. It was not her fault that the attempt failed. Her intention remained the same, the foul purpose of rousing the blood-thirsty Mohammedan world against Christendom, or rather against all Christendom except Germany. Nothing in the annals of the world has been more horrible than a successful *Jehâd*, and Germany believed that she was unchaining the hounds of hell when she inspired the summons to Islâm to rise against the infidels. If Islâm was more civilized than the so-called Christian nation that sought to rouse her, the credit belongs to Islâm. The shame remains to Germany.

Personally I hope never to witness a more revolting spectacle than that of November 13–14, 1914, when the proclamation of the *Jchâd* was publicly made in the Empire. In Syria there were harmless and unimpassioned demonstrations against the foreigners, the banners of Islâm were unfurled, and ancient battle-cries were faint-heartedly repeated with the shame-faced realization that the day of those sentiments was past, and that even to recall them was a disgrace in this generation. Along with those processions of pseudo-fanatics rode the German and Austrian representatives in Syria in full regalia; and from the same platform whence the Moslem orators exhorted their co-religionists to arise and exterminate the infidel, the German and Austrian consuls besought that same fanatical horde to unsheathe the sword against their Christian brothers. There was no apparent result from this propaganda, unless it be that it fanned the flame of Moslem fanaticism which later broke forth in the massacre of the Armenians. That it failed, let me repeat it, is to the eternal credit of Islâm. That it was ever attempted, should be remembered as Germany's supreme disgrace.

Our own American and English periodicals have already revealed to the public some of the subterfuges to which Germany resorted in the hope of ingratiating

herself with the Moslem world. I recall particularly
an article which appeared in the *Literary Digest* during
the first year of the war, in which was quoted Moslem
criticism of Germany's disloyalty to her professed
faith, Christianity. It was commonly believed among
the more ignorant classes in Turkey, and doubtless
elsewhere in the Moslem world, that the Kaiser was a
descendant of the Prophet on his mother's side—it is
enough to make the ghost of that English princess
walk!—and these same simple-minded folk believed
that Germany had embraced Islâm and had entered the
lists as a defender of the faith against the *Giaours*
(infidels). A vast number of Moslems were successfully duped, but the more intelligent, thinking classes
were only revolted by the insincerity and baseness of
the modern exponent of *Kultur*. It is a commentary
on the power of the Mohammedan religion that it fails
to satisfy an educated Moslem. Especially among the
Turks a man who has enjoyed the advantages of a foreign education, and who has developed intellectual and
ethical depths of character, is at heart more Christian
than Moslem. He may cling to the outward forms of
Islâm, may be regular in his attendance at Mosque on
Fridays, may even keep the fasts; but if he has truly
assimilated European ideals, he will probably have
only one wife, and will probably be open in his criticism
of certain formulas of the Moslem faith which he holds
are not adapted to the present stage of civilization.
Unfortunately for Turkey, however, men of this type
were in the political minority, and the infamous triumvirate at Constantinople had already elected that

Turkey should range herself on the side of the Central Powers in the world conflict. True patriots in Turkey mourned the certain destruction that awaited their country, but the Ottoman nation as a conglomerate mass had neither the wit nor the loyalty to understand or to care whither they were tending.

Among the influential classes in Syria, as well as Turkey proper, every man lived for himself, and every man's hand was against his brother. He who could snatched from those about him, and he who was robbed of everything laid himself down to die. Brother's hand was against brother, and son betrayed father. The rich ground down the poor, and those in power sacrificed the people to their selfish ambitions. Every one deplored the existing conditions, but not a single patriot arose to save the situation. There was no cohesion in the population. Christian distrusted Druze, and Moslem distrusted Jew. Because they would not hang together hundreds hung separately, and the Empire fell prey to the Germans and to Turks of the type of Talaat, Enver, and Jemal, who despoiled it without ruth.

Turkey's first act of defiance and self-assertion was the abrogation of the Capitulations, two months after the opening of the general European War, and one month before Turkey herself became a combatant. Under these Capitulations, as I have previously described, Turkey had for centuries writhed; but the civilized nations of the world had been inexorable, for they knew well that on them alone depended the peace and security of foreign residents in the Ottoman Empire. The agreement being bi-lateral could not be changed without the consent of both contracting parties; and, needless to say, the Great Powers had never consented to the least departure from the terms of the treaties. The abrogation of the Capitulations was part of the Young Turk program to shake off foreign tutelage and to create a new Empire on the basis of Turkey for the Turks. Naturally Germany encouraged them in this scheme of independence, realizing that it would only further Teutonic ends. It would be far easier for Germany to accomplish her purposes with Turkey if she were the sole sponsor, than if she were only one of several signatory Powers; and, of course, it did not take a diplomat to realize that Turkey must still depend on foreign support, at the price of concessions to foreign Powers. Accordingly, on October 1, 1914, the Sublime Porte decreed that the Capitulations were henceforth non-existent, and in so doing Turkey succeeded in directing toward herself the enmity of all Europe except the Central Powers. She staked everything on one hazard, Germany's loyalty; and Germany, as the world well knows, betrayed her at every opportunity.

A month later, November 1, 1914, Turkey and England went to war; and one after another the Powers of the Entente severed relations with Turkey and left her to her fate. This was a revenge far different from anything on which Constantinople had calculated. They had never taken it into their reckoning that for years the campaign against Turkey would be a mere side-issue, and that she would be cut off from the rest

of the world to starve, or to live on such alms as her
Teutonic patrons might, through motives of self-in-
terest, bestow upon her. For four years the ships of
the Entente fleets patrolled the Syrian coasts, but never
was there one serious attempt at landing. For four
years the enemy aeroplanes soared over the more accessible portions of the Empire; but if they ever
dropped a bomb, it was more as a pastime, to annoy
Jemal Pasha in some ostentatious passage through the
country, or to disconcert the Turkish troops assembled
for a special review. At times we revelled in the
omniscience of the Entente Powers, and chuckled to
ourselves when a French cruiser sent ashore a note to
the Governor of Beirût addressed and delivered to him
in Tripoli when he was there for a few hours only on
a secret mission unknown in Beirût itself; but as the
weeks dragged into months, and the months into years,
we grew heartsick with the suspense. Conditions in
the country grew more and more distressing. Disease
and famine walked abroad in the land; death and
nakedness stared us in the face, and the horror of it
all grew more than courage and sympathy could stand.
The Syrian people, after the first feverish weeks of
anticipation when they hourly expected an allied landing on the coast, at which time they themselves would
rise to join the invaders against the hated Turk, relapsed into dull apathy. All their time and energies
were devoted to satisfying the barest needs for existence, and if they gave a passing thought to the situation it was to curse the French for abandoning them to
their fate. Very soon even that vent to their feelings

was denied them, for they had before their eyes the
horrible example of some scores of their countrymen dangling from the gallows in the public squares
of the prominent cities of Syria—French sympathizers
and intriguers, apprehended by the Government and
doomed to a traitor's death.

V

THE ABROGATION OF THE CAPITULATIONS

IT was less than two centuries ago that Turkey, upon the declaration of war with some rival power, was accustomed to seize the diplomatic representatives of the hostile nation at Constantinople and immure them in the medieval dungeons of the Seven Towers. Even before the declaration of war between Turkey and England in 1914, the British Ambassador at Constantinople, Sir Louis Mallet, was threatened with assassination; and in the days which preceded the actual outbreak of hostilities it is said that he anticipated the possibility of imprisonment before he could leave the Empire. True to her traditions, upon the occasion of her entrance into the European War, Turkey took prompt steps to humiliate in every way possible any official representatives of the Allied Nations unfortunate enough to be trapped in the Empire at the time. This was especially true in the provinces.

I happened to be in Damascus on November 1, 1914, the day hostilities began between Turkey and England, and I was returning to Beirût on the train which carried the French, English and Russian consuls and vice-consuls from Damascus. Knowing that war was imminent, they had spent the last two or three days in

October in attempting to arrange with the Turkish
authorities necessary formalities preliminary to their
departure. All telegrams to and from their embassies
in Constantinople had been held up by the Turks for
several days past, and they were completely out of
touch with the trend of affairs. However, by Monday night, November 2nd, everything was arranged and
on Tuesday morning they boarded the seven o'clock
train for Beirût, whence they should embark by Italian
steamer. Once out of the Damascus station without
incident, I have no doubt each breathed a sigh of relief, and congratulated himself on his success. But
their satisfaction was short-lived. In its leisurely
progress over the ninety mountainous miles of road
to Beirût, the train reached Reyâk, the junction with
the Aleppo line, about noon. Here there was a customary halt of half an hour for luncheon, and most
of the first-class passengers alighted to take their noon
meal at the station restaurant. While we were eating
we noticed that several Turkish soldiers and secret
police had entered the restaurant and were furtively
regarding the foreign consular representatives. There
was little doubt as to what their next move would be.
Before they could finish their meal, the unfortunate
consular officials were taken into custody by the Turkish police and put into a train bound for Damascus.
It was only a prompt threat of reprisals from their respective governments that effected their release a few
days later, but they had to embark from Beirût like
fugitives on a stormy winter night in order to make
good their escape, as they well knew that the Beirût

authorities had been instructed to further hinder their departure in every possible way. Thanks to the prompt energy of the American Consul General in Beirût, Mr. Hollis, and of the Vice Consul, Mr. Chesbrough, they were safe on board the Italian ship, from which the Turks dared not remove them, when the Beirût officials awoke to their duties the following day. The Russian Consul General from Beirût was less fortunate. He was arrested and sent to the interior, and was subjected to such indignities on the way as only the Turks, inspired by the Germans, could stoop to invent.

The first problem which confronted Turkey after she had decisively committed herself for the war was the policy that she should adopt toward her resident enemies. There were thousands of enemy subjects scattered throughout the Empire, and the general fear on the part of the foreigners was that Turkey would pursue some " policy of frightfulness " in regard to them. She had before her the example of German brutality which struck a responsive chord in the cruel Turkish temperament. Only the facts that the majority of these belligerent subjects were now under American protection, and that Turkey desired the good-will of the United States, prevented the Turks from following their natural bent. America, moreover, had consistently refused to recognize the abrogation of the Capitulations, and insisted on the observance of her former treaty rights. The Germans, on the other hand, were using their utmost influence to induce the Turks to deal harshly with enemy aliens, particularly urging the advisability of detaining foreign residents as hostages for the good behaviour of their respective governments. Thanks to the efforts of the American Ambassador at Constantinople, most of the foreign residents of the Capital were permitted to leave the country, but those in the interior were never given such an opportunity. As long as American prestige proved effective there was no organized oppression of belligerents in the Empire; but as American influence gradually declined, and as German influence increased, conditions grew very serious for the subjects of nations hostile to the Ottoman Empire. Turkey was relapsing into that state of barbarism which was natural and congenial to her and which only the Capitulations had made impossible.

The next step on the part of the Ottoman Government was to seize foreign property and institutions wherever possible, and it was only the unflagging zeal of such American representatives in charge of belligerent interests in the provinces as the American Consul General in Beirût, Honourable W. Stanley Hollis, Consul Glazebrook of Jerusalem, Consul Young of Damascus, and Consul Jackson of Aleppo that thwarted the Turks in their intention of making a clean sweep of enemy property in Syria. In smaller places where there were no consular officials at hand, they broke into schools and even into private residences, and looted and destroyed without restraint. Most of the belligerent schools were occupied at one time or another by Turkish troops, who so befouled everything they touched that in some cases the buildings will have to be torn down and rebuilt before the premises can be used again as schools or as residences. For a time the representations of the American Ambassador at the Sublime Porte prevented this abuse of foreign property in larger centers, but little by little the aggressions of local officials increased, and their depredations, being apparently unmarked by the Central Government, became more and more unrestrained. By the end of the war there was probably not a building in the Empire which had belonged to belligerents which was not appropriated and converted into a Turkish barrack, a school, or an orphanage for the children of Turkish soldiers.

The British Consul General in Beirût, Mr. Cumberbatch, was far-sighted enough to realize as early as September, 1914, that it was no longer safe for British residents to remain in Turkey. He sent special messengers to the isolated localities where British subjects were living to bring them to Beirût, and about the middle of September he sent out of the country his family and as many Britishers as would heed his warning. He himself remained until early November, leaving only after the actual declaration of war between Turkey and his government. Unfortunately there were many British subjects who refused to leave the country, even though they realized that they were remaining at their own risk. None of them foresaw the possibility that the war would drag out for four long years. Many who had their entire capital invested in Turkey preferred to remain to look after their interests. A number of missionaries, also, refused to leave the field of their labours and the Syrians dependent on them. As far as I know, no other foreign colony was given a similar opportunity to depart before it was too late, and most of them paid bitterly for the lack of foresight of their representatives.

In December, 1914, the local officials in Syria and Palestine were instructed to deport the subjects of belligerent nations resident on the seacoast into the interior. When the order first reached Beirût, the American Consul General, Mr. Hollis, did his utmost through Ambassador Morgenthau to force the Sublime Porte to reverse the order. During the day or two while he was awaiting instructions from Constantinople, Mr. Hollis advised the British and French subjects, then under his protection, to keep out of the way of the Turkish police, and to avoid the issue until definite advice could be secured. Some two score or more French and British subjects living in Beirût took shelter in the compound of the Syrian Protestant College, which offered them an asylum until the matter should be definitely settled. There was an American cruiser, the *North Carolina,* in the harbour in those days, and every one knew that the Turks would make no attempt forcibly to remove any one whom the Americans had made up their minds to protect on their own premises. The word came back from Constantinople that even belligerents connected with American institutions, or under American guarantees, must leave for the interior, but that women and children would be exempt. The Turks, wishing to draft for military service the graduates of the Syrian Protestant Col-

lege Medical School, exempted also three British doctors who were important men in the medical department. The Constantinople newspapers subsequently
commented on the fact that Turkey had thereby forced
British subjects to contribute toward the Turkish military campaign!

On December 9, 1914, the first deportees, a forlorn
little band of British, French and Russian subjects,
with here and there a Belgian, or a subject of one of
the Balkan kingdoms, were packed into the train and
taken to Damascus, where they were held as civil prisoners. In the beginning they were not badly treated.
They were permitted to live in hotels, or even in
private houses; and were required only to report at
the Police Station for registration once a day. However, there were many hardships to be endured by
those who were thus exiled, especially as at one time
they were in the position of hostages rather than mere
interns, when Jemal Pasha threatened to exact reprisals on them in connection with a British naval
demonstration against Alexandretta. Families were
separated, the men being taken into the interior, and
the women being left in their former residences to
suffer the most wearing anxiety due to mistrust of the
Turk. Old men and sick men were taken, as well as
men of military age; and some that went to live in the
interior went practically penniless, as the order came
so suddenly that they had no time to prepare for the
journey. One of the most sickening days of my whole
life in Turkey during the war was that immediately
preceding that deportation. Several members of our

little Anglo-American community came into the American Press, where I was working, to leave in American hands their wills, their valuables, and their final instructions. As we accepted their commissions and wished them Godspeed, we tried to smile, but we dared not look into those haggard faces, for fear the tears that lay so near the surface would overflow.

Of those that went into exile that dreary December morning some never returned, but were buried in the interior. The majority were held nearly four years as civil interned prisoners until shortly before the signature of the Turkish Armistice on October 31, 1918. Only some few drifted back, largely through the efforts of friends who had influence in Constantinople. About a dozen were released from Damascus on December 22, 1914, arriving in Beirût in time for Christmas; and they were permitted to remain until April 5, 1915, when they were again deported, this time until the end of the war. After a great deal of wire-pulling, certain elderly men, or men useful to the Turks, such as the Belgian Director of the Tram Company, the French Manager of the Electric Company, and others, were finally granted a permanent exemption.

There is no space here to tell the story of the exile of those belligerent friends of ours; but, no doubt, some one of them may himself one day give his story to the world. Suffice it to say here that later the women also were deported to Aleppo, with the exception of a few whose physical condition even the Turks recognized as too delicate to permit them to make the journey. Later all the belligerents, men, women and children, were deported even further into the interior, to Urfa, in the Mesopotamian Valley. Here they witnessed all the horrors of one of the two Armenian massacres before the women were transported to the seacoast at Alexandretta, whence they were removed by an American cruiser. After the second massacre of the Armenians, the men were returned to Anatolia and were scattered in isolated and out-of-the-way Turkish villages about Konia, Sivas and Angora. The life of these men, who knew no Turkish in these Turkish-speaking towns, who were cut off in many cases from all communication with their relatives and friends, and who were subjected to the thousand and one petty annoyances, insults, and dangers, the invention of which so delights the Turkish provincial official, can only be left to the imagination. Indeed, after the Armistice it was almost as if the dead had come to life at the trumpet-call of the new era. Young men grown old, old men with tottering steps and childish minds, good men grown evil, and evil men grown brutal, arose from their long imprisonment and reappeared in the world of the active. Some of us, who were either more hopeful or more ignorant than the rest, had deplored the hopeless pessimism with which these same men had left our midst four years before; but that tragic roll-call when they reassembled convinced us, even if the events of the past four years had not already done so, that they were wiser than we in dreading the future which placed them at the mercy of the Turk's brutality.

VI

THE AMERICAN RED CROSS TO THE RESCUE

AS Americans our position in the Empire was unique, and for some time indeed enviable. Diplomatically we had enjoyed the privileges of the "most favoured nation," and practically that was exactly our position during nearly three of the four years of the war. The reasons for this were several. Turkey undoubtedly realized early in her alliance with Germany that she must not look to her ally for material financial support; and like many another impoverished nation, she began to speculate on the possibility of diverting to herself some of America's immense wealth. Politically also she was in desperate need of a friend; and she fondly hoped that the sympathies of America, the great neutral nation, might with a little diplomacy be enlisted in her behalf when the final day of reckoning should come, and when Turkey should have no other friend at the peace-table to champion her cause.

We only dimly realized these things in the early days of the war, and wondered that we as Americans enjoyed so many privileges. American consular representatives were allowed to affix their official seals to certain of the buildings belonging to the British which the Turks were most anxious to seize and occupy, and for months those seals were left intact. American official interference in behalf of belligerent subjects was tolerated in a way that surprised us, and for several months after the withdrawal of the British missions from Syria, the American Press was permitted to continue the salaries of their native employees in accordance with lists received by what we called " the underground mail route." This latter form of relief, however, soon became too dangerous to be continued, as the Turks pretended to look with suspicion on such transactions, which might be interpreted as British propaganda and the support of British agents. It was more for the safety of the Syrian employees of the British missions than from any concern for the Press itself that these payments were eventually discontinued, although the result was that many of the valuable Syrian teachers and assistants in other departments of the mission work, all of whom had been educated and supported by the British missionaries, died of disease and starvation during the absence of their patrons from Syria.

Encouraged by the apparent good-will of the Ottoman authorities, the American community of Beirût determined to inaugurate a campaign against the distress prevalent throughout the country. The organization was ready to hand. There was existent a five-year-old Chapter of the American National Red Cross (the first ever established outside of the United States or its dependencies), founded at the time of the Armenian massacres of 1909. By the time that the Beirût Red Cross Chapter had decided to undertake active relief-work, Turkey was in reality at war with England, France and Russia, and the country was already afflicted with all the misery which in most cases exists only as a direct result of active military campaigns. But even had Turkey not actually entered the arena, the Chapter would have felt amply justified in making plans for relief-work which could be truly defined as an attempt to "mitigate the suffering caused by . . . great national calamities, and to devise and carry on measures for preventing the same."[1] That was in the early days of American Red Cross activity in connection with the European War, before the tremendous drain upon the resources of the organization made it necessary for the National Society to adopt the resolution that its funds should be used solely for European relief for sick and wounded of the armies of all nations then at war.

In December, 1914, the Beirût Chapter of the American National Red Cross held its annual meeting and elected officers for the coming year. Honourable W. Stanley Hollis, the American Consul General at Beirût, consented to serve as President of the Chapter. Professor James A. Patch of the Syrian Protestant College was elected Vice-President; Mr. Dana, Manager of the American Press, Treasurer; and myself, Secretary. Three additional members were elected to the Executive Committee: Mr. Bayard Dodge; Mrs. H. G. Dorman, and Mrs. H. H. Nelson, all of the Syrian

[1] *Red Cross By-laws.*

Protestant College. Later Professor Robert B. Reed, in charge of the Employment Department for Men, and Miss Anna Jessup, director of the same work for women, were invited to become associate members. At the end of the following year political conditions in Syria were such that it was impossible to call the regular annual meeting of the entire Chapter, and it was informally agreed that the same officers should continue to serve. In compliance with the request from the State Department in Washington that consular officials should not hold office in Red Cross Chapters, Mr. Hollis resigned, and Mr. Patch was elected President. Professor J. Stewart Crawford of the Syrian Protestant College then became Vice-President. The Executive Committee comprised this personnel during the full term of its service in connection with the Great War; and even after the cessation of the activities of the American Red Cross in Syria, certain members of the former Executive Committee continued to serve on what is now known as the Permanent Committee for American Relief in Syria. In other words, the members of the Red Cross Executive Committee were in charge of all the relief-work that was accomplished in Syria with American funds during the last five years. To them belongs the credit for the truly remarkable achievements of American philanthropy during this dark period, and to-day they are still held responsible by the charitable organizations at home for the proper administration of the funds.

At the December, 1914, meeting, the Chapter empowered the Executive Committee to direct the work of investigation of local needs through poverty and suffering; to appoint sub-committees, including Syrians; and to administer all funds with a view to promoting the general usefulness of the Society. The Executive Committee formulated its campaign along two distinct lines of relief: first, the preparation and dispatch of a Hospital Expedition to the Fourth Ottoman Army Corps in the campaign against Egypt; and second, the organization of a local relief-committee to minister to the immediate distress among the civilian population of Syria. The civilian relief-work was organized in three departments: employment, flour-distribution, and assistance to the families of Ottoman soldiers in obtaining from the Government the promised allowance for support.

An appeal for funds was forwarded to the National Headquarters in Washington, and a prompt response came in the form of $10,000. This amount was supplemented from time to time; and by November, 1916, the Beirût Chapter had received from Washington an aggregate sum of $33,641.55 for relief purposes. This sum was further augmented by considerable private donations and by large grants from relief-societies all over the world. In the autumn of 1916 the Armenian and Syrian Relief Committee took over the support of relief-work in the Ottoman Empire, and in January, 1917, made a grant to Syria of $50,000. An additional $700,000 was invested in food and clothing to be dispatched as a Christmas present to Syria from the American public. Two days in October, 1916, had been appointed by President Wilson as gift-days for Armenia and Syria, and America had responded generously to the appeal.

The responsibility for the organization and management of the Medical Relief Expedition was entrusted by the Executive Committee to the Faculty of the Syrian Protestant College as a sub-committee for medical relief. Under their able direction a hospital unit was organized and equipped. This was accepted by Jemal Pasha, the Commander of the Fourth Ottoman Army, and the agreement was that the unit should serve as a tent-hospital of two hundred beds at Hafir el-Aujah, a station on the Egyptian frontier, one day's ride from Beersheba. Dr. E. St. John Ward, Professor of Surgery in the Syrian Protestant College, was appointed director of the expedition, and Rev. George C. Doolittle of the American Mission, associate director. The rest of the staff consisted of Dr. Naimeh Nucho, pathologist; Dr. Athman Saadeh, assistant pathologist; Dr. Atiyeh, assistant surgeon; twelve seniors from the Syrian Protestant College Medical School as orderlies; two pharmacists, one dentist, and four sisters of the Kaiserswerth as nurses, making a staff of twenty-four. In the preparation and equipment of the hospital unit all the labourers were furnished by the Employment Bureau of the local relief-committee. The expedition carried with it a fully equipped operating tent, and a pharmacy tent supplied with a three months' stock of medicines. The expedition left Beirût on January 21, 1915, and proceeded safely to Hafir el-Aujah, where the hospital was established. They remained two months, returning to Beirût March 27th. During the time of their service they treated about two hundred and twenty patients. The fact that this number is so small is not a commentary on the efficiency of the hospital unit, but is a revelation of conditions in the Turkish Army. Of that ill-starred expedition very few survivors ever returned. The Turkish forces were practically wiped out. Those that escaped the British bullets succumbed to disease and starvation in the desert. Many bands of stragglers either lost their way in the wilderness, or perished in the terrible sandstorms which overwhelm the wandering traveller. Of those who were wounded in the campaign only the merest handful received medical aid at the front, and none but the hardiest could survive the dreadful two-days journey on camels to the Red Cross hospital at Beersheba.

On May 4, 1915, the Beirût Chapter received an urgent appeal from the American Ambassador at Constantinople for the immediate services of a hospital unit to aid in caring for the wounded of the Gallipoli campaign. The Ambassador offered transportation for the party by the U. S. Collier *Vulcan,* then in Turkish waters. The Beirût Chapter voted to send the expedition, and the Syrian Protestant College generously agreed again to liberate Dr. Ward, together with Miss Van Zandt, and Miss Nightingale, nurses in the College Hospitals. The party left on the *Vulcan* May 16th, and remained in Constantinople until August.

By the middle of May, 1915, only five months after the commencement of organized Red Cross work in Syria, when the annual report of the Beirût Chapter was submitted to the National Headquarters in Washington, the hospital unit to Beersheba had been dispatched, and had returned to Beirût. The second hospital unit was on its way to Constantinople, and the local relief-work was proceeding in smooth-running order. Arrangements had been made in coöperation with the municipality for the employment of able-bodied men in a crusade for cleaning and repairing the streets, and in a general campaign of sanitation. The city had been plotted out in twelve districts, each under the supervision of an American woman, members of the College or Mission communities; and in each of these districts, after careful personal investigation by the district superintendent, a list of worthy candidates was prepared. Flour, a week's portion at a time, was doled out to those families of destitute women and children who had no wage-earners to support them. Later a Women's Employment Bureau was instituted, with special emphasis on lacemaking and needlework for which there was always a good sale.

The relief-work in Syria was centered in Beirût for two reasons: the Central Committee was located there, and the Beirût Chapter as such was directly responsible to the National Committee in Washington for the proper administration of the funds appropriated to Syria. Moreover, there was a greater need in Beirût and its immediate vicinity than in any other one locality. Obviously a crowded city presents more problems than the rural districts, and the situation in Beirût, a city dependent on commerce and trade, was more desperate than that in such a city as Aleppo, or Damascus, which are centers of internal economy. Beirût was the gathering-point for the destitute of the country for miles around. Immigrants from Lebanon who had been starved or frozen out of their former homes flocked to the city in the hope of finding work there. It was estimated at one time that there were as many as forty thousand homeless and destitute people in Beirût who had assembled there from all over the country. The funds at the disposal of the Red Cross workers were limited, and it seemed wiser to do a little thoroughly than to attempt too much and accomplish little for want of concentration. Appropriations were, however, granted from Beirût to other cities, among them Ḥomṣ, Tripoli, Sidon and Tyre, Damascus, Ḥaifâ and one or two of the larger villages in Lebanon, to be disbursed according to the judgment of the Americans resident there. In most of these places the work was conducted along practically the same lines as the work in Beirût.

The work of the Red Cross proceeded smoothly until August, 1915, when it was suddenly terminated by an open exhibition of hostility on the part of the Turkish authorities. The Governor of Beirût, Azmi Bey, had made no secret of the fact that he had been chafing under what he considered the impudent interference of the Americans in civil and municipal affairs. He had undoubtedly been awaiting the opportunity to strike in a way that would at once cripple the Red Cross activities and humiliate the American personnel. It matters not that the nominal aggressors were underlings, minor police officials. None of them would have risked his position in such a move had he not been certain of the temper of his superiors. The blow fell suddenly and took the form of the arrest of Mrs. Dale, Superintendent of the American College Hospitals in Beirût. She was directing the relief-work in her district when the police arrested her together with several of her Syrian assistants. They were conducted to the central police station, where they were detained until the personal representations of her brother, Dr. Frederick Bliss, effected her release. The matter roused a storm of feeling both on the part of the Americans and of the Syrians who had benefited by their activities, and who felt that their very lives depended upon the continuance of the Red Cross work. However, the matter being thus brought to an issue, the Governor expressed himself emphatically as antagonistic to any such usurpation by foreigners of his own prerogatives, and the Red Cross was forced to discontinue its work in the Beirût municipality.

In Lebanon, however, the Governor, Ali Munif Bey, took an entirely different attitude, and intimated that he would be not only willing but grateful, if the American Red Cross might transfer to the province under his jurisdiction the relief machinery which had operated so effectively in Beirût. He stipulated merely that the Red Cross should consent to a nominal coöperation with a committee of the Ottoman Red Crescent created for the purpose, which comprised a group of men so tolerant and so acceptable to the Americans that the most cordial relations were possible between the representatives of the two committees.

The Red Cross Executive Committee elected as representatives to the joint relief-committee Mr. Patch and Mr. Crawford from the College, and Mr. Dana and Mr. Doolittle from the Mission. The leading spirit among the Red Crescent representatives was Judge Mohammed Effendi Abou Izzedine. His death from typhus during the winter of 1917 proved a serious blow to the relief-work in Lebanon; so much was his heart in the undertaking that during his last illness he worked in bed over the details of organization as long as his strength permitted, and in his delirious ravings he lamented over the suffering in Lebanon which weighed so heavily on his mind.

The joint relief-committee continued to operate for five months, from December, 1916, to April, 1917, when America entered the war. Mr. Doolittle took up his residence in Ba'abdâ, the seat of the Lebanon Government, in charge of the relief-bureau there, but the other members of the Red Cross committee were obliged to make several trips to Ba'abdâ each week during the worst winter weather. I shall always have a vivid memory of these gentlemen, clad in rubber coats and high boots, setting out in the rain on their cold, dismal journey to a committee-meeting in the mountain village an hour distant. They travelled frequently on foot, occasionally by carriage, or on horseback.

The meetings of the full Beirût Executive Committee were continued all through that winter, as the four representatives to the joint-committee were not empowered to act without specific instructions. Every important project was reported to the Executive Committee before action was taken, and the representatives were instructed in detail as to their policy in any vital matter. This seemed necessary as a safeguard against possible machinations on the part of the Turks.

The relief-work in Lebanon was carried on along much the same lines as the work in Beirût, and for several months the Red Cross Chapter was privileged to direct an enterprise which gave vent to the energies and sympathies of its members. Anything was better than being idle at a time of such great distress!

In the autumn of 1916 the Armenian and Syrian Relief Committee announced that its Christmas present to Syria was a shipload of food and clothing, which was to be transported to the Syrian coast by the U. S. Collier *Cæsar,* under the consent of the Allies and the guarantee of safe conduct from the Germans and the Austrians. For about three months the Beirût Committee, in collaboration with the Red Crescent, turned all its wits and energies to preparing for the arrival of " the Christmas ship." Warehouses were secured, arrangements completed for docking and unloading the precious cargo and guarding it against possible attempts at confiscation by the Beirût authorities. The Red Cross Executive Committee, of which I was then secretary, held three and four hour sessions three evenings each week over the knotty problems connected with safeguarding the relief supplies from the moment of their arrival until they were delivered to the most needy Syrians outside of Beirût, and yet accessible from Beirût. From the very outset we had determined that the *Vāli's* attitude precluded any possibility of aiding Beirût's residents, and we resolved that we would make a serious issue of the question rather than allow one grain of wheat to fall into the granaries of the corrupt officials of the Beirût municipality.   More than one thousand villages in Lebanon were personally visited by Red Cross agents and lists of needy individuals were made up in three categories in order of need.   The plan was so perfected that immediately upon the arrival of the *Cæsar* the cargo could be unloaded and distributed to centers where detailed lists of candidates for relief were in readiness.

The expected arrival of the ship had been generally advertised by the American and European newspapers circulated in Syria, and also, indirectly, by the special preparations devolving upon the joint-committee for relief.   The whole country was literally living on expectation.   One of our community met an old man coming out of a bakery holding in his hand the " chalk and alum and plaster   .   .   .   sold to the poor for bread."   He was shaking his head over the unappetizing and unnutritious lump and muttering to himself, " Bad bread to-day, bad bread to-morrow; the next day the American ship comes."   What then happened was the greatest tragedy of the war in Syria.   You in America perhaps know better than we just why the Christmas ship never came, although we are only just beginning to apprehend the political complications which spelled death and disaster in Syria, and sore heartache for those of us who had given months of our time and thought to the successful execution of this project.

The ship reached Alexandria safely; and as soon as its arrival there was reported in Syria, every one expected that it would reach Beirût without further delay. But it never reached Beirût! Its arrival was postponed from week to week, and from month to month, until one day the whole country awoke to realization of the fact that it was never coming. The failure of a ship to reach port is one of the most familiar tragedies of life. Shakespeare has vividly interpreted for us in *The Merchant of Venice* what the loss of a vessel means to an adventurous business man who has invested his full fortune in its cargo. The whole world turns sick with horror over such a catastrophe as the loss of the *Titanic,* or the sinking of the *Lusitania,* each with its precious freight of human life. In these days of mammoth vessels such a disaster means the death of hundreds, or even thousands. But the failure of the *Cæsar* to reach Syria meant the loss of tens of thousands. The official statistics for the month succeeding the announcement that the sailing had been cancelled show a higher rate of mortality than any other one month during the war. Literally hundreds died of disappointment. It had been a case of " while there is hope there is life." Thousands had been living on scanty rations with the expectation that a day of comparative plenty was ahead. Others had borrowed against the time when they might repay by sharing their rations from the *Cæsar's* cargo. When they at last realized that the ship was not to come and that their credit was no longer good, their last hope for the future set; they had no further courage to live, and nothing to live for. Oh, the tragedy of that bitter disappointment! I must confess that we who had given so much of ourselves for the success of this enterprise of American philanthropy and Christmas good-will felt that we had been deserted by the home-committee and left to cope unaided with the desperate situation in the land to which we had pledged our support. We now know that it was not the fault of either the Relief-Committee at home, nor of our Government. Once again Syria, and particularly the civil population of Syria, had been the victim of international politics.

In April, 1917, the breaking of relations between America and Turkey placed the Americans in the Empire in a position practically amounting to that of belligerents, and with the loss of our neutral status the possibility of overt humane service was closed to us. The Beirût Chapter of the Red Cross continued to operate in a quiet way until it had expended the funds in hand at the declaration of hostilities, but in June, 1917, it held its last meeting. From then onward until the end of the war a local relief-committee, financially backed by the personal guarantee of the members of the American Mission, continued the philanthropic service, although it was necessary to revise the whole method of procedure.

VII

THE AMERICAN MISSION PRESS IN A NEW RÔLE

THE peculiar exigencies of such a crisis as the recent World-War have submitted institutions as well as individuals to an analysis which has lowered the mighty and exalted the humble. Many a respected citizen has proved himself a "slacker," and many a town "tough" has covered himself and his community with glory. Fortunes have been made and lost in a day in war speculations, kings have been elevated or cast down. Business-houses with a long-established reputation have forfeited public esteem by their conduct during the national crisis; and others have sprung from obscurity to world-prominence. The general call to arms inaugurated new standards of value. In these last five years men and institutions have been rated according to their relation to the vital issues at stake, and not with regard to their pre-war status. It is as if the war had destroyed the whole existing order, and created a new era with new standards. The missionary who, perhaps, previous to the war, was ridiculed for the eccentricity of his appearance, or his absorption in the problems of a remote foreign locality, has now been called to advise with those empowered to determine the fate of nations.

On the other hand, the potentate who was powerful enough to plunge the whole world into turmoil is to be tried as a common criminal; and while his fate is yet undecided, passes his days felling trees on an estate in Holland.

In this general social and commercial upheaval the American Presbyterian Mission-Press at Beirût has known its share of the radical transformation. What was five years ago an obscure mission printing-house has to-day international recognition not only as a commercial and banking institution, but also as a relief-center similar to a charity-bureau in one of the great American cities. The soul of the enterprise has been transfigured, and yet its physical appearance is the same. Even the face and form of a man alter as his mental and spiritual capacity increase, but the American Press is still lodged in a building which gives no hint of its internal transformation. From a dingy office in a patchwork building, which was once the Mission-Church, the Press Management directs transactions which involve annually the manipulation of millions of dollars. In this building are housed the Treasury of the American Presbyterian Mission in Syria, and of all the relief-societies operating in Syria; the financial correspondents for Syria of the Standard Oil Company of New York; the agents of the American Bible Society; not to mention another tremendous commercial and financial enterprise. And yet the name painted over the door is simply *The American Press,* and even this brief title is popularly clipped to *the Press.*

Experience has taught that one of the vital factors in successful mission-work is a mission printing-house, inasmuch as it is always possible, even in countries where large public meetings are forbidden, to reach the literate masses through the printed page. The American Mission in Syria was no sooner established than the need of a mission-press made itself evident. Conditions in the Ottoman Empire, however, were such that it seemed inadvisable to attempt anything in the line of publication at that particular time, in view of the fact that the Turkish censorship of printed matter was fanatically rigorous. In 1822 the Congregational Mission Board at Boston determined to locate the American Mission-Press for Syria in Malta, until such time as conditions in the Turkish Empire would permit of its transfer to Asia Minor or Syria. Twelve years later the opportunity came; and in 1834 the Press was removed to Beirût, where it has operated for eighty-five years with only one interruption. This was during the war between Turkey and Russia in 1853–56, when the American missionaries fled for a few months to Cyprus for safety, at which time the translation and editorial work of the Press was likewise carried on there.

The greatest modern literary contribution to the Arabic-speaking world—which comprises one-fifteenth of the population of the globe—is the Arabic version of the Bible, translated and published by the Beirût Mission-Press half a century ago. This has been repeatedly revised and modernized; but in spite of the enormous demand from all parts of the world for the

Scriptures in Arabic, the American Press is the only printing-house in the world which produces the complete Arabic Bible in all forms. In addition to religious literature of all types, the American Press has translated into Arabic and publishes school-books, fiction, and miscellaneous works on scientific subjects; and many of its publications are circulated throughout the whole Arabic-speaking world. During the year 1913, the Press exported to the United States, South America, India, Egypt, Africa, Mesopotamia, Arabia, and the islands of the Pacific more than 200,000 volumes of its productions.

The Press has never lost sight of the fact that it must keep pace with Syria in its growth and development. As education has become more widespread throughout the country, there has been an increasing demand for clean, interesting and instructive literature in Arabic to compete with the immoral literature translated from the French which has lately flooded the market. Not only must the Press increase the quantity, but also the quality of its output. At the outbreak of the European War plans for a new and modern building were in hand, and the Management was concentrating all its energies on the problems of how, and along what lines, it might increase the staff, both editorial and administrative, so as to meet the needs and grasp the opportunities of the age.

It will be necessary to digress here to sketch briefly another phase of the Mission-Press activities which was unofficial, but vitally important to the American Mission community in Syria, and which in a measure explains why the Press was called upon, during the war, to play so large and so varied a rôle. The American Mission in Syria is centered in four stations, Beirût, Sidon, Tripoli, and Zaḥleh in Lebanon, from which centers the work in the out-stations is directed. Of these four cities Beirût is the only one that occupies a position of commercial importance. Sidon and Tripoli are not large ports in the sense that they are suited by their location for extensive maritime operations. Neither has a harbour, but Beirût can boast one of the few fairly good harbours on the coast of the eastern Mediterranean. Zaḥleh, on the other hand, lies far in the interior—far, that is, for Syria, where ten miles present greater difficulties in travel than one hundred miles in America or Europe. Beirût is the seaport for Damascus, and consequently for the whole interior as far north as Aleppo. At Beirût the ships of commerce discharge their freight, and through the Beirût custom-house eighty per cent. of the imports to Syria pass. Obviously, Beirût station is the Mission's point of contact with the outside world, and in Beirût the Treasurer of the Syria Mission must be located. The Manager of the American Press is, therefore, also the Treasurer of the Mission.

The result is self-evident. A missionary in one of the other stations sends to America or to England for a consignment of groceries. Will the Manager of the Press please, as a personal favour, send some one reliable to the custom-house to clear the said consignment, and see it safely dispatched by train to Zaḥleh, or by cart to Sidon or Tripoli? Of course, the Manager cannot refuse so reasonable a request, but in the course of a few months the Press is obliged to develop a regular shipping-department with a complete staff that devotes practically all its time to questions concerned with customs, transport to the interior, and kindred problems. Similarly, in compliance with orders from all parts of the country, the Press keeps a special employee to make purchases in the Beirût shops, which are, of course, superior to any in the interior; another to be responsible for the quantities of mail for the out-stations which come directed to its care. The Press, being located in the metropolis, has facilities for cashing checks and handling accounts in banks that have no provincial agencies. The Manager of the Press, being on the spot, can reserve steamer-passage for the missionary starting home on furlough, or meet the incoming steamer and pilot the new arrival past the greedy customs officials to hotel quarters previously engaged by the Press. In short, the American Mission-Press is the Cook's Agency, and the Import, Export, and Purchasing Office of the Mission, merely because it is the only American institution in Beirût with a staff sufficiently large to warrant the assumption that " there will surely be some one to spare who can do just this for me."

Not only the American Presbyterian Mission in Syria requires these special services of the Press, the same is true of every mission in Syria and Palestine, from the Taurus Mountains to the Egyptian border. The mail of a single day brings to the Manager's desk orders ranging from a slate-roof for a new school-building four hundred miles to the north of Beirût, to a horse and buggy for a missionary on the edge of Ḥaurân, or a tombstone for a grave in Damascus.

With this established precedent, it was no abrupt departure for the Press gradually to assume more and more obligations of a financial and commercial character; until with the war's continued embargo on trade, and the impossibility of securing necessary printing-supplies, the publication side of the Press's activities diminished in proportion as the financial side increased. The paralysis of the business world and the suspension of normal trade activities has already been discussed in a previous chapter. Banks were closed and all communication with the outside world ceased, save through the Ottoman Post Office and under the eye of the Turkish censor. The Press, however, arranged an " underground " mail-route, the only channel which permitted of freely-expressed correspondence with the outer world. General, unimportant mail was entrusted to the local Turkish Post Office as a blind, for its total absence would immediately have aroused suspicion. This " underground " mail-service was available for only a few months; but brief though the period was in which the Press could communicate freely with its home-board, the Presbyterian Board of Foreign Missions of New York City, it was sufficient to establish in America a firm understanding of the situation in Syria and of the needs. In the light of this understanding subsequent correspondence passing through the Turkish Post Office might be so cryptic as to be unintelligible to the censor and yet be perfectly comprehensible to the correspondents. Through the medium of the "underground" a numbered letter was forwarded by the Manager of the Press to the Treasurer of the Board requesting the latter to deposit the sum of One Thousand Pounds with a certain bank in Switzerland to the credit of the account of the American Press. Six months later, the Turkish censor would not find anything startling in a cable phrased as follows: " Repeat transaction my number eleven, two instead of one "; and yet it would have a very definite message for the Treasurer in New York, meaning this time that he was to deposit with the Swiss Bank Two Thousand Pounds for the Press account.

In December, 1914, Mr. Dana, the Manager of the Press, cabled Mr. Dwight H. Day, his New York Treasurer, to accept for transmission to Beirût any sums of money which Syrians in America might wish to send to their relatives in Syria. Upon receipt of lists of amounts deposited in New York, together with the names of the sender and the payee, the Press guaranteed to make payment in any part of Syria. This step was taken by Mr. Dana purely as a relief-measure, and he little suspected the proportions to which it would very shortly develop. In less than a year the Press had paid out more than $2,000,000 to approximately 30,000 Syrians living anywhere in the country, from Gaza, near the Egyptian border, to Bagdad in Mesopotamia. The difficulty of locating and identifying the thousands of payees living in isolated villages scattered throughout this vast region was indeed tremendous, but it was accomplished with a very slight increase in the staff of workers, and without the loss of a dollar through mishap or mispayment.

During the summer of 1915 this relief-work on the part of the Press and Mission had become so extensive, and such a large proportion of the population depended upon financial assistance from the Americans, that the Turkish authorities began to display open hostility toward the work. Our chief enemies among the Turkish officials were Azmi Bey, Governor of Beirût, and Muhhedin Bey, Chief of Police, both of whom were notorious assassins, and both of whom were agents of the Triumvirate in Constantinople in their scheme for the deliberate extermination of the Syrian people. These men recognized in the work of Mr. Dana, as Manager of the Press, and his resultant contact with the Syrians an important obstacle to their plan of exterminating this subject race as effectively, but not so conspicuously as they had exterminated the Armenians. Furthermore, he was handling immense sums of money, portions of which they believed they might divert into their own pockets, if only they could sufficiently intimidate him or threaten the suspension of his work. In other words, they were determined that his work should continue only if it were sufficiently remunerative to them.

In the accomplishment of their purpose, there was nothing to which these two men would not stoop; and when overt methods failed, they resorted to blackmail and intimidation. Their first attempt was to cut off the Press from its mail, in the hope that, if they could

prevent the arrival of the weekly packets of instructions from New York, the " remittances to Syrians,"
as we at the Press designated them, might be terminated. The next line of attack was to accuse the
Press of making payments to the Syrians in behalf of
the British and French Governments with a view to
purchasing the promise of Ottoman subjects to join the
enemy at any moment when Entente intervention
might appear imminent. Another charge was suggested by the jealousy of the local banks, namely, that
the Press interfered with the business of legalized
banking institutions, which, it was said, had been
forced to suspend operations because they could not
compete with charitable organizations. Finally, the
Manager was personally accused of manipulating the
Turkish paper-currency in such a way as to cause its
depreciation to only one-fourth of the gold value. All
of these charges were, of course, absolutely false.
The Press had always played fair with the Government and had never transgressed any of the laws of
the Empire. In particular, the last mentioned charge
was not only unjustified, but positively contrary to
fact. The Press was in reality the greatest agency in
Syria for upholding and stabilizing the value of the
Turkish banknotes; and had it not been for the financial prestige of this one institution, paper-currency
throughout the country would practically have gone
out of circulation, as it did in all isolated localities in
the interior not affected by our financial transactions.

During the last three years of the war, Mr. Dana's
life was one of constant annoyance and danger. The

infamous Azmi and Muhhedin combined forces to intimidate him by false accusations, threats, and secret intrigue. Day and night he was dogged by spies who watched his every move with greedy eyes in the hope that some indiscretion on his part might deliver him into their hands. Scarcely a week passed that he did not receive, either in a personal interview, or by an anonymous letter, some threat or warning of blackmail. The arrival of midnight telegrams was so frequent an occurrence as to cause no alarm in the Dana household, but time and again we were roused in the dead of night by a terrific pounding on the door which proved to be no telegraph-boy but some of the most dastardly agents of the police. On several occasions Mr. Dana was summoned forth at midnight to secret police quarters in the town where he was interrogated, threatened, and pressed for money until he could convince his enemies that neither the fear of death, nor the more horrible things that they threatened could induce an American to sell his honour.

On one occasion he was roused from his sleep, and conducted by two non-uniformed spies to a building near the Police-Station. Here he was told that the charges which had been lodged against him and which were then under consideration by the Chief of Police were so grave that only the payment of a large sum of money could save him. They flatly demanded $10,-000; and when given a positive refusal for even a small amount, one of the men left the place under pretence of reporting to the Chief of Police the failure of their negotiations. The second man proceeded then to enter into a violent discussion with another person whom Mr. Dana has always supposed to be an Armenian who had been alone in the dark room when the American and his two captors had entered. As the conversation was conducted partly in Armenian and partly in Turkish only a word now and then was intelligible to Mr. Dana, but it was evident that this was a similar case where money was being demanded. Finally, when the threatening rage of the Turkish spy could apparently wring nothing from the victim, the Turk seized the wretched man by the neck, stabbed him twice through the breast, then cut his throat. The murderer, sprayed with the spurting blood, threw the knife on the floor and turning to Dana said in Arabic, " He has refused to pay the money demanded." The American was evidently intended to understand that he might expect a similar fate if he too persisted in his refusal.

Later the assassin disappeared and returned after having changed his clothes. He reported that the Chief of Police wished to buy a check on Dana's New York bank, and would give him the countervalue in cash a few days later. The check, however, must be delivered that very night. They apparently wished to change slightly the colour of the blackmail procedure to a commercial transaction, but the Manager of the Press knew that the money would never be forthcoming. There was no way out of the situation save through apparent acquiescence. He was taken by the spy to the Press, where he wrote a check on a New York bank that was unnegotiable. This, however, entirely satisfied his Turkish tormentors. As soon as the check was delivered over he was allowed to return to his house, but he lived in daily suspense of their discovery of the ruse. He was slightly relieved when a few weeks later the Chief of Police, the head of the three conspirators, came to an untimely end. Six months later the second was brought low by a British bullet on the Palestinian front. The third still haunted him like a spectre of death for nearly two years, although Mr. Dana never knew whether he had discovered how they had been outwitted. Eighteen months later he appeared again in the dead of night on the wide ledge outside the window of Mr. Dana's hotel room. His appearance was a great shock, for Dana had no idea that he was still dogging him.

*　*　*　*　*　*　*　*　*　*

The next morning the local papers mentioned the discovery, in an alley beside the hotel, of the corpse of one of the old Hamidian spies. He was lying on the edge of the pavement with his skull crushed, and had apparently fallen from a great height. The Greek tenants of a third-story apartment directly across from the hotel were at first suspected, as it was known that this man had on several occasions ascended to their rooms, as he said, " to make observations." The Greeks were subsequently exonerated, but the police evidently never discovered how the man had met his death. The incident was in itself a frightful one, but the death of the one remaining man who had been involved in the blackmail attempt and who had been outwitted through the trick of the bogus check, closed forever a fearful chapter of suspense and terror in Mr. Dana's life.

In such a country as Turkey it matters little whether a charge be true or false. It is not the innocence or the guilt of the accused that determines the outcome, but the comparative wit of the contestants. In dealing with barbarians only primitive methods avail, and the victory is to the keener cunning. In Turkey a murderer with a sufficiently strong following may live in security, and even occupy a position of honour and influence. But a righteous man who has powerful enemies is doomed to destruction, unless he be constantly on his guard, and unless also he be subtle enough to keep his own counsel, and sufficiently wary to foresee and forestall his opponents' moves. In the case of the Manager of the Press, it was one man against a whole corrupt administration, and I cannot believe that mere human wit saved the day. Something more than tact and insight was essential in the conflict of honour with infamy, and civilized principle with barbaric brutality. Personally I can only believe that this struggle between American philanthropy and Turkish lust of destruction was only another phase of the world-conflict of civilization against barbarism, of right against might. It was with this faith that we fortified ourselves in those soul-racking days. Here in Syria we were fighting our share in the World-War just as truly as were our compatriots on the Western Front.

Although we never confessed it even to each other,

I am certain that we of the Dana family had no more expectation that Mr. Dana would live to see the end of the war than we should have had, had he been assigned a particularly dangerous post in France. And yet we should have been " slackers " had we used our influence to induce him to leave the country, or to give up the unequal combat. There were times when it seemed physically impossible that the human mind could bear such a strain as was constantly put upon him, and even those of us who know him best and who shared most intimately his life during that dreadful period cannot fully comprehend what inherent force of will, or superhuman coöperation gave him strength to win through safe and sane.

A few months ago, while travelling on the train from Cairo to Port Said, I met a British officer of twenty-one who wore on his right sleeve five chevrons, one red that showed he had volunteered for service during the months of 1914. On his left sleeve were two vertical gold bars. Presuming upon that peculiar intimacy which sometimes arises during companionship on a long journey at the end of which one knows lies a parting of the ways, I asked him to tell me where he had been fighting when he was injured. There was something strikingly impersonal in the frankness with which he then related the episode in France in which he had been wounded. He had been struck, and had fallen in the path of a machine-gun which peppered him with bullets as he lay unconscious on the ground. During the thirty-six hours that he lay in " No Man's Land," he had received six wounds, each of which might have proved fatal, had it been located a hair's breadth to one side or the other; and yet not one vital organ or one essential muscle had been destroyed. He was nine months in the hospital, during three of which he had neither memory nor consciousness. When he finally returned to his regiment, he was another man, a man who had walked into the very jaws of death, and who looked thenceforth upon every day of his life as a privilege beyond his wildest imaginings. I doubt whether that youth will ever know fear again, or will ever lose that sense of unexpected richness in the possession of life. I asked him later what he was particularly interested in. "Oh, everything!" he exclaimed, as much as to say, "Who would not be, who might be lying in his grave in France, were it not for a miracle?"

As my young uncle, Mr. Dana, listened to the story of that youthful hero, I saw in his face the reflection of the other's mood. He too had dwelt in daily companionship with death, and had even felt its awful clutch. He too was still alive to work, to play, to be "interested in everything." And in the faces of both I read something else that I could not name: perhaps a fresh purpose in life, and the resolution to make the most of it while it lasted. Certainly it was not the "eat, drink and be merry" attitude. Far from it! Rather the conviction that a life which had been so miraculously spared had perhaps been spared with a purpose, and was, therefore, in a measure consecrated to a cause,

VIII

SYRIAN PHILANTHROPY FROM ABROAD

FOR those of us who worked at the American Press during the period of the war there remain three impressions of vivid drama: tragedy, pathos, and comedy. "Remittances to Syrians" is the official title in the books of account of the American Press of that extensive line of business which provided the means by which Syrians living abroad might send money to relatives in their native land. The accounts and records of the Press reveal such bare facts in connection with this relief-work as have already been enumerated in the preceding chapter: statements of the amounts received, by whom they were sent, and to whom they were to be paid. It would, however, have been impossible to devise a system by which one could become more intimately and more extensively acquainted with the life of a nation than by this.

The system in itself was beautifully simple, but its success was due entirely to the loyal coöperation of numerous agents, notably the Treasurers of the Syrian Mission-stations in Lebanon, Tripoli and Sidon. The Press is under no less a debt of gratitude to other assistants, not of the Mission, but one with the Mission in their whole-hearted enthusiasm and coöperation with such work as the Mission was attempting, through the Press, for relief in Syria. It would hardly be fair to mention one or two without naming all, and it must suffice here to state that these agents were located throughout the whole country: in Jerusalem, Ṣafed, Damascus and Aleppo in the interior; in Jaffa, Ḥaifâ, Latakia, Mersina and Alexandretta on the seaboard; and in numerous towns in the interior of Anatolia and even Mesopotamia. Every one offered his services free of charge, as his contribution to the relief-work. The regular staff of the Press in Beirût, whose work had been considerably lightened through the decrease in the activities of the printing-department, was transferred almost bodily to this new department, thereby reducing to a minimum all expenses in connection with administration.

Early in January, 1915, an advertisement was inserted in all the Arabic and many of the English newspapers in the United States announcing that the Treasurer of the Presbyterian Board of Foreign Missions would accept for transmission any sums of money which Syrians resident in America wished to send to their relatives in Syria. This notice was copied by Arabic newspapers all over the world with the result that in a few months money was pouring in from all quarters of the globe to the Board's office in New York. It was soon necessary to employ a special staff to handle the work at the New York end. The money was received either in the form of postal orders, or checks which had to be negotiated through regular banking channels, or wads of American greenbacks paid in over the desk of the receiving cashier. Receipts were issued to the depositors, and notification slips bearing the name and the address of the payer and payee in Arabic and English were prepared at the same time in New York. These slips were later given to the stenographers, who made up lists reading as follows:

" Inclosed find check for $1,525.60 to cover the following remittances:

$50 from Yusef Touma, 116 Broad Street, Canton, Ohio, to his mother, Sobat, in Deir el Kamr, Lebanon,

$40 from Hanna Haddad, Washington Street, New York City, to his brother, Khalil Haddad, a shopkeeper on the Beirût River Road, Beirût,

and so on through a list of fifty to one hundred items, some of them far less explicit in their instructions. These lists were dispatched weekly to the Treasurer of the Syria Mission in Beirût, who gave them first his careful personal attention, and then turned them over to his secretaries, who " routed " them, that is, separated the items and relisted them according to the districts in which they should be paid. In such a list as that quoted above of, say, one hundred items, forty-one might be paid from the Beirût office, nine in Lebanon Station, twenty-one in Tripoli, seven in Sidon, and the remaining twenty-two scattering payments in Jerusalem, Nazareth, Ḥaifâ, Aleppo, Antioch and Mardin. To each disbursing center was dispatched the list of payees living in that locality, the money with which to make the payments, and in some cases typewritten receipts all ready for the payee's signature. At stated intervals, the signed receipts were turned back to Beirût, where they were classified and filed according to districts and villages.

As I said, the system was simple, in fact could hardly have been simpler, but there were countless difficulties involved in successfully carrying it out. The greatest problem, apart from the never-ceasing hostility of the Government, lay in securing the money with which to meet these orders for disbursement. It was out of the question, for several reasons, to consider transferring funds from New York to Beirût, as rates of exchange were prohibitive, and banking-business was at a standstill. After moderately successful attempts in various directions, Mr. Dana finally discovered that the most satisfactory method was for him to sell checks on his New York bankers in exchange for Turkish paper-currency. During the three years when this method was in practice, the average rate was about $3 to the Turkish Lira instead of the par rate of $4.40. This slight gain on exchange enabled the Press to meet expenses of administration in connection with the Syrian remittances, and still disburse at a trifle above par, a gain which was of but slight value to the recipient, but which gave the lie to subsequent accusations that the Press was growing rich by unlawful profit on exchange.

For example, the dollar at par was worth twenty-two and one-half Turkish gold piasters. At times when exchange rates were particularly favourable the Press paid out as high as thirty-five to forty paper piasters for each dollar. The relative value of gold and paper was not proportionate to the exchange values, but, nevertheless, it is a matter of considerable pride to the Press that while amounts transferred through the local banks lost in transit as much as eight per cent., ten per cent., and even twenty-five per cent. and thirty per cent. of their face-value, amounts transferred through the Press gained a maximum of sixty per cent.

I have gone thus completely into what is a purely technical question for the reason that the Press has been subjected to a vast amount of unjust criticism from Syrians abroad who have been advised by their relatives and friends out here that sums sent through the Press have suffered enormous depreciation. This is true only in so far as Turkish paper had depreciated in relation to gold. One hundred dollars deposited in New York would, at par, have been worth £tq.[1] 22.50, but was paid in paper by the Press, when rates were favourable, at £tq. 30. If these £tq. 30 were exchanged into gold only £tq. 6 could be purchased, the equivalent of $26.40. It is evident that the $100 has lost $73.60 in transit, which is true in so far as its purchasing value was concerned. As a matter of fact, the payee gained over the par rate $33, the difference between £tq. 22.50 per $100 and £tq. 30 per $100. As gold was outlawed by the Ottoman Government and was confiscated wherever it could be discovered, it could not be circulated by the Press without jeopardizing the interests

[1] £tq.=Turkish Liras.

of its tens of thousands of beneficiaries. The Press, however, always gave the payees the option of refusing the sum outright, in which case it was returned to the sender without any charge for transfer; or of delaying receipt on the chance that rates might take a more favourable turn. Because, as I said, there has been a great deal of unintelligent criticism of the Press's methods in financial matters, I have risked boring the average reader for the sake of enlightening those who are interested in this phase of the question from the angle of the business man.

The whole work, however, has not been one of business, dull and prosaic. It has presented a most fascinating opportunity for contact with Syrians of all classes and all walks of life, both in their own country and abroad. There was scarcely a transaction that did not have its humour, its pathos, its tragedy, or its dramatic side; and none that did not amply repay the effort involved with the realization that through the hand-to-hand exchange of money there was the heart-to-heart exchange of sympathy. Who would not labour early and late, with infinite anxiety, and even danger to his own personal safety, if thereby he might be the agent of salvation to those menaced with death by starvation, nakedness, and exposure? Who of us has seen some dull countenance brighten with new hope at the almost forgotten sight of money, or felt on his hand the kiss of gratitude, mingled with tears of emotion, without thanking God for the generosity of those Syrians overseas who, by their economy and the sacrifice of legitimate and hard-earned comforts, spared the wherewithal to keep alive their brothers in Syria! How often we have said to each other, " If only the man who sent that amount could have seen the joy in the face of his relative here when he received it!"

I must take this occasion to express the profound admiration and affection for the middle-class Syrian, more especially the country-folk, which grew up in me during the years of the war, as a result of my contact with them through this Press relief-work. Their family loyalty and their willingness to share with each other even the last crust is something so beautifully touching that I have felt humbled before it. I have known a man of moderate means, who supported his whole hamlet of perhaps fifty persons as long as his own income held out, and who died the same death from starvation as did the others when his funds were exhausted. There is a man in the village where we spend the summer who maintained during the war a family of fourteen individuals, some of whom we should term " distant relatives," although it meant that he and his own family of five must forego all the comforts, and even many of the actual necessities which he might otherwise easily have provided for them.

After working, day in, day out, on the lists from New York, one comes in time to realize that Rosa Haddad in Fall River, whose address indicates that she is a day-labourer in a big shoe-factory, is sending a monthly remittance of $10 to her old father in Lebanon; and I have tried to read between the lines of those matter-of-fact records from the New York office of names, addresses, and amounts, the sacrifices and even tragedies that those lists represent. Perhaps Rosa drew upon the little fund that she had laid aside for her trousseau when she should marry Habeeb, and she bravely determined upon the postponement of her wedding, even before Habeeb received the letter from Shweir announcing the death of his brother and the fact that their crippled sister, Jameelie, would follow him to the grave unless Habeeb could contribute toward her support.

The Syrians abroad rose as one man to the assistance of their countrymen. The economies and dreams of a lifetime, the hope of a comfortable old age, or a triumphant return to the native land as a wealthy foreign resident were none too precious to sacrifice in such a time of need as the period of the war. I, for one, shall never see a rugged mountaineer without remembering that he may be such a hero or the father of such heroes as those I have just described. I shall never look into the sad face of a young mother, toiling along a dusty road with her child in her arms, without wondering whether in her home she has mothered other chicks besides her own. It matters nothing that there have been men of the so-called upper classes of society in the country who have done their utmost to disgrace the name of Syria before the nations of the world—robbers, usurers, and land-grabbers. A nation is as good as the best of its people; and the country that can produce the every-day heroes and heroines that the war has developed in Syria is worthy of honour at home and abroad. Many a demoralized city-dweller has lived a life consistent with the standards of the decadent society of the later Roman Empire, or of France during the Reign of Terror. But as long as there lives in Lebanon a race of sturdy mountaineers with the sturdy virtues of a mountain people, Syria will and must develop into a strong nation.

One phrase has been constantly on American lips when Syrians have attempted to express their heartfelt gratitude for their preservation. "You must not thank us. You must thank your own people, in America, in England, in Egypt. It is they who have sent the money that saved your lives. We Americans have been only the agents to see that it reached you." It is, however, heart-warming and to the missionaries must seem the culmination of a century's labour, that relations between the Americans and the Syrians have during the war become so cordial. We have never done all the things with which they credit us, but perhaps it is inevitable that there should be a strong bond between those who have together experienced such hardships as did all who continued in Turkey throughout the whole period of the war. The facts that the Americans, no less than the Syrians, were at the mercy of the Turks, that they too knew anxiety as to where they should obtain the winter's wheat-supply, that they denied themselves all possible luxuries, that they ate the Syrian dishes, and wore clothes made of native fabrics—in short, that they lived just as the Syrians lived—these facts perhaps place them in a peculiarly intimate relationship with the Syrian people. Every American who remained in Turkey after the departure

of the official representatives in April, 1917, did so
with the knowledge that he remained at his own risk.
Disease, starvation, and complete isolation from his
home and friends in America were actualities at the
time when he made the decision, and there were yet
more dreadful possibilities ahead whose full horror
only the Turks could realize.

I dare write thus frankly of the heroism of the
Americans with whom I was associated because of my
own peculiarly sheltered position.   In one sense, I was
almost a bystander, and the sorrows that darkened
those dreadful years were for me purely vicarious.   I
never knew any personal uneasiness, for I was in no
way in the public eye, but I was saddened with anxiety
for the safety of my uncle and his family.   I was
young, and had none dependent on me.   I was free
to go or to come without concern as to how my move-
ments would affect those whom I loved.   I had only
an indirect share in the work that the Americans were
doing in the country; and therefore, I may be par-
doned, if what I say of my countrymen expresses my
pride in them, and I may at least be exonerated from
the suspicion of personal vanity or self-satisfaction.

All over the world men and women have eased their
breaking hearts with the hope that " somehow good
will be the final goal of ill," and in Syria to-day we
are fortunate in that we can already see some of the
beneficial results of the ills which we have survived.
We should have sufficient cause for gratitude were our
only gain Syria's liberation from the oppression of the
Turk, but there are improvements of a more subtle

character which are evident, probably, only to one who knew the country before the war as well as after. From the missionary standpoint, the greatest step toward progress has been the tendency to merge sectarian enmities in a rapidly growing national loyalty. There is, furthermore, a gratitude to America which has been expressed at times in a most astonishing way.

For generations the French Catholics have been exceedingly jealous of American religious influence in the land, and they have instilled into their converts much of their intolerance and bigotry. The fact, however, that the American relief-agencies made no distinctions of race or creed in their service to the Syrian people disarmed hostility in a most surprising way. The Americans were fully aware of the bitter enmity of the Catholics (locally known as Maronites), especially in that Kesrawan region of Lebanon, north of Beirût. That knowledge, however, was no deterrent when it came to the possibility of rendering relief to the Maronite inhabitants of this district, which suffered particularly from the effects of the war.

While writing this I chanced to turn over the figures showing the totals of the various sects helped by America's charities during the last two years of the war. Out of 46,000 Christians who received relief, fifty-four per cent. were Roman Catholics and Maronites, and only one and one-fourth per cent. were Protestants. More than that, even the priests, hostile as they had always been toward the American missions, were glad to avail themselves of the privileges of receiving money through the Press, and of banking there.

The Press stood ready to deliver money to any individual lucky enough to have relatives abroad desirous of thus assisting him, and never inquired whether he were priest or layman, Mohammedan, Druze, Greek Orthodox, Protestant, or Maronite. Some of our most satisfactory dealings were with the Maronites; and if some of our greatest annoyances were caused by the priests, that was no more true of the Catholics than of the priests of other sects. The Syrians have a saying that, if you wish to find the Devil, you have only to lift the cap of a priest; and there were times when we were tempted to believe the truth of that malicious proverb. As a matter of fact, most of the flagrant cases of dishonesty and falsehood must be laid at the door of the clergy; and one or two typical incidents will reveal what we had to contend with.

Mr. Nejib Kheirallah, the paying cashier at the Press, fortunately for the Press, was a young man of rare shrewdness, otherwise our proud record of no losses through mispayments could never have been attained. On one occasion a priest entered the office and presented one of our regulation notices which requested Mikhail Gabriel to call at the American Press on important business. Such notices bore only the name of the payee and the serial number of the payment. The name of the sender was omitted for a special reason. In Syria, where family names are a comparatively recent achievement, it frequently happens that there are two or more men of the same name in one village, just as it might happen that there would be several George Henrys in Paterson, New Jersey.

It would, however, be a rare coincidence if two of these Syrian George Henrys had relatives of the same name residing in the same place in America. The prospective payee, therefore, is required to give the names of relatives or friends residing abroad from whom he might possibly receive an amount of money; and if among those names should occur the name of the actual sender, the identification is practically complete. Of course, further safeguards in the way of written guarantees from the *sheikh*, or mayor, of the village in which the candidate lives, reliable witnesses to the signature, *etc.*, are required.

This priest presented the notification slip, and announced that he was Mikhail Gabriel, and that he had come to get his money. There was something odd in his manner, and Nejib Kheirallah looked searchingly into his crafty face. However, as his answers to the usual questions tallied with the information forwarded from New York, and as his credentials from the *sheikh* and other dignitaries of his village were in perfect order, there was no reason for withholding the payment. Like a hawk, however, the cashier scrutinized his every move, and the moment that the priest set pen to paper to affix his signature to the receipt a slight tremor betrayed some unusual excitement. In a flash the cashier had him by the throat, and, worrying him as a dog worries a rat, accused him of forgery. The man turned ashen white and fainted from terror. When he came to, he confessed his guilt and pled for leniency. Mikhail Gabriel had died only the week before, and the priest had intercepted the Press notice with the intention of securing the money for himself. Had he been the only individual involved, his prayer for mercy might have been granted, but the matter was too serious to be lightly dismissed. In his hands Mr. Kheirallah held the written evidence of the perjury of the *sheikh* of the village, and the other " reputable citizens " who had borne false witness to the man's identity. The case was put in the hands of lawyers, and the criminals brought to justice. Investigation revealed forty inhabitants of that village whom the priest had unsuccessfully approached in his attempt to secure by bribery the necessary guarantees.

A delightful contrast to such an incident was the visit which the Manager received from other priestly representatives from a distant monastery high up in the Lebanon Mountains. A delegation called upon him to express their gratitude for the assistance rendered through the medium of the Americans, and to discuss the possibility of their recording their appreciation in some more substantial form. They had determined to present President Wilson with a desk made of the fragrant cedar-wood, requesting him to accept it in recognition of the gratitude of the Syrian Catholics for the generosity of the American public. It was a beautiful idea, and the Manager assured them that President Wilson would undoubtedly treasure such a gift; but at that time it was impossible to think of sending to America anything so bulky as a cedar-wood desk. The priests were disappointed, but promised to reopen the question after the war. It may be that some day they will; if so, I trust that the President

of the United States will value the token as one that
is truly significant of a change of heart on the part of
at least certain representatives of a class that five years
ago was the most bitter enemy of the American Mission.

One would have to write a book of several hundred
pages to do justice to the human side of this relief-
work.   A thousand and one nights would not exhaust
the treasury of stories of incidents that have made us
laugh and weep.   You would have forgotten for a
moment even the most pressing care, if you could have
heard Mr. Dana laugh, when, in reading over the lists
of instructions from New York, he came to an item
of $100, "to be delivered with a thousand kisses to
my sister in Jerusalem"!   Your heart would have
been lightened of a load of sympathetic anxiety when
you discovered on another list a substantial sum for
the poor woman who had waylaid Mr. Dana a week
before as he passed through a remote mountain-village,
and who had poured into his ears her pitiful story.
Her daughter lay ill of typhus, and she had no money
for medicines or proper food.   She had only sufficient
flour for one more baking.   Was it an answer to
prayer that her son in America, from whom she had
heard nothing for ten years, was suddenly inspired to
send her a sum of money?

But the tragedy of the sums that came too late!
One day a doctor from a village on the coast north of
Beirût came into the office to receive about $1,400
which he was charged to distribute among the residents
of his village.   There were about thirty names on the

list forwarded to him by the senders. He wept as he read it over, and he told us that only five of that thirty were still alive.

On other occasions money came as a perfect God-send, and relieved an otherwise desperate situation. Mr. Assad Kheirallah, the Syrian guide, philosopher, friend, and secretary of the Press, was making a tour through the Kesrawan region of Lebanon. It was winter, and he had besought the Manager to allow him to make the journey to some of the more isolated villages to deliver the money, rather than require the poor people to take the long journey to Beirût to obtain it. Darkness had overtaken him at a wayside inn, and he had taken shelter there for the night. He had scarcely touched the hot supper that his host had prepared for him when there was a shuffling of feet at the door and two men entered bearing the apparently dead body of a scantily clad man. Good Samaritans that they were, they had picked him up from the roadside where they had found him, and brought him to the inn with the hope that warmth and nourishing food might save his life. He revived more speedily than they anticipated, and when he was strong enough to talk he told them that he had walked down to the coast from one of the highest villages in that district of Lebanon only the day before. All winter he had struggled to keep himself and his family of four motherless children alive, but he had finally reached the limit of his resources. He had sold everything in the house from the kitchen-utensils to the beds on which they slept. He could borrow nothing, for his neighbours were as poor as he was.   He could not remain in the house and watch his children starve under his eyes, so he had bidden them farewell, and departed for the coast in search of assistance.   He had little hope that he would meet with succour of any kind; and when he left them he had determined that he would not return if he must go back empty-handed.   His benefactors heard his sad story, but they themselves were poor, and had nothing to give.   Mr. Kheirallah, who had not spoken before, then asked the man his name; and when he heard it, began asking the most curious questions.   Have you any relatives in America?   Where do they live?   What are their names?   At first the poor man could recall no kinsman living abroad, but finally he recollected the fact that his brother's youngest son had gone away some years before, and the last they had heard had been living in Providence, R. I.   Mr. Kheirallah inquired his name, and then consulted his list.   There was a sum of $200 for the man before him from this almost-forgotten nephew!   The man could not believe his good fortune, but was finally persuaded that the money was indeed his.   He did not know how to sign his name on the receipt, but he made his thumb-print over the stamp, and the next day he returned to his village with sufficient supplies and money to see him and his family through the remainder of the winter.

Up to the date of writing, the records at the American Press show more than a million individual items disbursed to persons of all classes and creeds in Syria. About one-third of these are the so-called " Syrian

Remittances," forwarded by the New York Treasurer.
The remainder represent items sent through the American Embassy, the Swedish Legation, the Dutch Legation in Constantinople, the American Diplomatic
Agency in Cairo, the American Consulate General of
Beirût, a Jewish relief-society, and numerous private
charitable organizations.   There is hardly one of
these but bears mute testimony to similar incidents.
The Governor of Beirût was not far wrong when he
recognized in the work of the American Press a formidable obstacle to the Turkish program of destruction; nor was he mistaken when he feared that it would
result in a sympathy between the Syrians and the
Americans which would only further emphasize the
contrast between American and Turkish methods of
procedure.   His worst fears were being realized; and
finally, in a truly Herodian fashion, he determined to
remove the man whom he considered his most effective
opponent.   How he did so, is a chapter by itself,
and will be dealt with as such; but it was not until he
had tried every other plan of interference and oppression that he finally resorted to such a drastic measure
as the removal of the director of the whole relief-work.

In May, 1917, the Press was given a warning hint of
trouble ahead when Assad Kheirallah, the most powerful Syrian in connection with American influence in
the country, was made the victim of a fresh scheme of
Turkish vengeance and injustice.   Mr. Kheirallah, together with quite a number of other prominent Syrian
business-men, was deported to Adana.   The alleged
reason for this unprecedented move was the determi-

nation of the Ottoman Government to deal summarily with those who were said to be responsible for the Syrian lack of confidence in the Ottoman banknote. The Turkish paper-currency issues were daily depreciating because of the evident demoralization of the government. Mr. Dana's name had also been on this list for deportation; but through the timely intervention of Syrian friends, it had been removed just before the "round-up" was made. The list also included the name of another most valuable friend of the American Press, Mr. Joseph D. Farhi, a prominent Jewish business-man who had secretly negotiated hundreds of thousands of dollars' worth of American Press drafts in securing funds for relief and for the general finances of the Press and Mission.

Four months after Mr. Kheirallah's departure into exile, Jemal Pasha was paying a visit to the village in which the Kheirallah family lived. Mrs. Kheirallah and her daughter went to call upon him, stating plainly that it was purely a business-visit for the purpose of laying before him the injustice that had been done the head of their house. They stated emphatically that they were asking only for justice, and they requested an investigation. They said, " If you find Assad Kheirallah guilty of anything against the Government, we should be the first to urge his punishment. If you find him innocent, we are sure you will promptly return him to his home."

Jemal Pasha was overcome with surprise. He had been besieged with requests and petitions, but never one from two women who so fearlessly demanded of him justice in its highest form.   He saw that they were unusual women, educated, refined, and dauntless. He promised them on his word of honour that he would look into the matter at once; and if facts were indeed as they represented them, would act promptly. Within a few weeks Mr. Kheirallah was home, and was never again molested by the Government.

During the whole period of the war practically all of the difficult, and even dangerous questions between the American Mission and the Turkish Government were handled skillfully and successfully by Mr. Kheirallah. The whole American community is convinced that there is no one like him in all Syria, and it would be impossible to express in words the gratitude due one who has endeared himself to all his countrymen, whatever their creed or political persuasion.

IX

UNJUST STEWARDS — PERSONALITIES IN REGARD TO CERTAIN TURKISH OFFICIALS IN SYRIA

AN account of life in Turkey during the Great War which did not include more than a passing reference to certain prominent Turkish officials would be like the proverbial production of Hamlet with Hamlet left out; or more properly speaking, a melodrama without a villain. Around such figures as Enver Pasha and Talaat Pasha in Constantinople, Jemal Pasha, Azmi, Muhhedin, Tahsin, and Bedri, Beys in Syria, the whole action during this period is pivoted; and without them one could no more make a reader understand why life in Syria was what it was than one could relate the life of Christ without mention of Herod and Pilate, or describe Rome of 65 A. D. without an exposé of the character of Nero. Indeed, I can only designate such personalities as Jemal Pasha and Azmi Bey as anachronisms. Personally I could not be in the presence of either of them for a minute without being almost terrified with the realization that here was a man that did not belong to this generation, or to this stage of the world's civilization.

Behind the dapper exterior of the Europeanized Turk, modern to the last mode in dress and social manner, smouldered the barbaric brutality of bygone centuries. If ever there was an argument for the re-incarnation of human personalities, that argument is Jemal Pasha or Azmi Bey. It is easier to believe that the uneasy spirit of a Herod or a Nero has been reëmbodied in one of these modern Turks than it is to consider them the product of the present era. It seems incredible that the twentieth century could produce such types, and still more incredible that even in Turkey they should be rulers with unlimited powers, rather than criminal outcasts.

Constantinople has never been veiled from international gaze as has Syria, and the careers and personalities of such men as Enver and Talaat have been familiar to the world at large ever since the birth of the Young Turk party in 1908. Moreover, they have been so ably depicted in *Ambassador Morgenthau's Story* that it is hardly necessary here to do more than touch on them in their relation to Syria. Talaat Pasha never figured directly in Syrian affairs, yet it is a known fact that the same fiendish cruelty which originated the idea of the Armenian massacres was also responsible for the attempted extermination of the Syrian race. He was the leading spirit in the Triumvirate at Constantinople, and admittedly the power behind the throne. The unexpected advertisement of the Armenian atrocities, however, taught the wily Talaat a lesson, and in the direction of affairs in Syria he took pains that his responsibility should be screened behind his tools and accomplices actually in Syria. He succeeded to a certain extent because one who knows the villainous Azmi feels it unnecessary to search further for a man sufficiently wicked to devise such fiendish cruelties. Azmi was undoubtedly responsible for the specific details, but it is unquestionably true that Azmi could not have retained his position one day had his administration not been harmonious with the program drawn up in Constantinople.

Enver Pasha, a young, good-looking man of the people, who had risen through sheer arrogance and through successfully executed assassinations, who had married a sultana, and lived in luxury in a palace on the Bosphorus, was at the zenith of his meteoric career during the war. In his capacity of Minister of War, he made three flying visits to Syria: one to Aleppo during the planning of the Mesopotamian campaign, one to Damascus to assist in adjusting a difference between Liman von Sanders and Jemal Pasha, and one to Jerusalem and to Beirût in order to satisfy himself to what extent Jemal Pasha was playing fair with his Constantinople party. There had been considerable apprehension on this score at the Capital, because it was known that if a good opportunity arose Jemal Pasha would intrigue with the Entente.

That last visit remains very plainly in our memories as the Beirût flour-supply was curtailed for three days previous in order that on the day when Enver arrived the city might be flooded with bread. Bread was for the first time distributed to the poor people gathered at the municipal soup-kitchens just before Enver arrived, and the happy crowd was photographed by the visiting party. As soon as Enver left that quarter the bread was snatched away by the police from the starving people, many of whom died from the shock of the disappointment, and was hurried to another soup-kitchen where it was used in the same way. Needless to say, the report reached Constantinople that Beirût was plentifully supplied with food, and that the poor were being well cared for by the municipality; but Enver probably laughed up his sleeve for he knew the real conditions.

It was during my year's residence in Constantinople that Enver became a reality to me, for I frequently saw him there. The fact that he lived in constant terror of assassination only served to advertise his presence and herald his trips about the city. On several occasions the tram on which I was travelling to the city from Arnaoutkeuy on the Bosphorus was delayed for nearly an hour at the gate of Enver Pasha's palace. All traffic in the streets was habitually suspended along the route from his home to the War Department in Stamboul, and secret-service men were stationed every quarter of a mile along the way. The Pasha travelled in a large closed touring-car which raced through the streets at a speed that would rival that of a New York fire-company, and when the car was still blocks away the incessant shriek of its siren could be heard above the din of the city. There was something awesome in the sound, and the reckless pace at which the car was driven typified the brute terror of the owner who chose to risk the lives of a cityful of people rather than travel at a speed which might expose him to an assassin's bullet.

Unlike Talaat and Jemal, and indeed the majority of Turks in public or private life, Enver was wholly inaccessible to a woman. It is a curious fact that the Oriental, for all his contempt for womankind in general, will seldom refuse an interview to an individual woman. The Turk, whether he be cabinet minister, provincial governor, or director of a commercial concern, will grant a woman requests which a man would not dare to utter, especially if she can summon to her aid a few melting tears. But Enver Pasha, for reasons only suspected, was possessed with the fear that he would meet his death at the hand of a woman, and not only was no woman permitted to approach him on matters of business, but he shunned society and divided his time between his own well-guarded home and his equally well-guarded office in the War Department.

Enver was the special tool of the Germans, and I know from personal experience that practically the only way to gain his ear was through the good offices of Germans connected with the Embassy or attached to the Turkish War Department.

While the personalities of Talaat and Enver are vividly imprinted on my mind, nevertheless my knowledge of them is second-hand, and such as any American might have who had followed the course of events in Turkey for the past ten years. When it comes, however, to Jemal Pasha and Azmi Bey, the protagonists in the war-drama of Syria, I feel that I am qualified to speak with far more certainty and assurance.

Not only did I see both of these men frequently, and even in the case of Jemal in a social way, but my own life was shadowed with the horror and anxiety which even indirect contact with such devilish personalities inspired. I am fully aware that certain members even of our own American community have spoken in defence of these men, but in all such cases it is easy to trace the reason in the fact that they were the recipients of very marked favours in the way of patronage and special privileges. The Turks realized that by granting such favours they themselves would eventually profit, directly or indirectly. There were several periods during the course of the war, particularly after the breaking of relations between the United States and Turkey, when the very existence of such institutions as the Syrian Protestant College and the American Mission schools was extremely precarious. The Turks were already in possession of the property of all belligerent institutions, and they were devoured with longing to assume like control over American property. The situation was an extremely delicate one, and one which called for consummate tact and diplomacy. Fortunately our American Ambassadors to the Sublime Porte during this period, Mr. Morgenthau and Mr. Elkus, were richly endowed with both of these necessary qualities, but there was so little coördination between the Government in Constantinople and the provincial officials that a point once settled in principle in the Capital might, nevertheless, cause constant difficulty and annoyance in the provinces. Such a matter as the collection of taxes on the property of foreign institutions, for instance, had been theoretically settled for all time when the Capitulations were formulated; but when, after the abrogation of these treaties, the matter was again raised, the Sublime Porte stated in positive terms that American institutions were still to be exempt. Even such a definite statement of policy, however, on the part of the Central Government did not prevent the frequent resurrection of this old cause of friction. Time and again charges for taxes were presented to the American institutions, and time and again the matter was referred to Constantinople and the previous decisions reconfirmed. The same was true of questions connected with special permits for individual schools operated by the Americans under one general, blanket firman (or imperial permit), from the Sultan; likewise of the exemption of pastors and teachers from military service, and other matters no less vitally connected with the existence of American educational institutions in the Empire. As long as there was an Ambassador in Constantinople, there was only one course of action for the Americans to take, namely, the reference of their problems to their national representative at the Capital; but after the departure of the Ambassador in 1917, all such issues could only be settled locally, and by the exercise of tact and persuasion. Although American interests had been confided to a neutral government, our treaty rights were not sufficiently understood by this to give us adequate protection. Moreover, the Swedish Legation was avowedly pro-German in sympathies, and in many cases where the Germans were at the bottom of some particular unpleasantness, the Swedish Minister refused to act against the interests of his Teutonic friends.

The Turks naturally took advantage of our defenceless position to stir up many old causes of grievance in the hope that they might either enrich themselves by the sale of favours to the Americans still resident in the country, or that they might come into possession of certain much coveted properties in Syria such as the American College in Beirût and the American Mission property in the out-stations. Obviously, there were two courses for the Americans to follow: that of ingratiating themselves with those in power, and thereby obtaining immunity from aggressions; or that of adhering staunchly to what had been in the past the American national principle in dealing with the Turks, whatever the cost might be in loss of property or interference with established activities. The Syrian Protestant College took the former course, and the American Presbyterian Mission the latter, and it is somewhat of a commentary on the undependability of the Turk that subsequent events proved that each course brought results practically contrary to what might have been expected. It might almost be laid down as a general principle that concession to one demand from the Turks brought another on its heels, while a firm refusal frequently " called their bluff."

The foregoing remarks, though merely a hint, may serve to explain the fact that two Americans resident in Syria under the régime of Jemal Pasha and Azmi Bey may give entirely contradictory reports as to the true nature of these much-talked-of men. The College was the recipient of many favours from both, and doubtless feels honour-bound to temper its criticism accordingly. The Mission, on the other hand, suffered particularly at the hands of the local governors, as it was firmly determined not to yield in the smallest detail to what it considered unreasonable demands, especially when compliance with such demands might bring into question its loyalty to its own government. The American Mission had come out to the country to serve the Syrian people; and while the missionaries respected the laws of the Ottoman Government, and conscientiously endeavoured to render unto Cæsar Cæsar's due, and never overstepped their treaty rights, their sympathies were frankly with the subject race; and wherever possible they used their influence in behalf of the oppressed. I doubt whether they had even vaguely formulated the theory of a nation's right to self-determination before President Wilson gave utterance to his famous " Fourteen Points," but the merest humanity compelled coöperation with those who were in distress, even though that policy might result in open conflict with the oppressor. On the other hand, the maintenance of over-cordial relations with the Turkish authorities seemed to some Americans to border on treachery to their own government and disloyalty to their Syrian protégés.

Jemal Pasha was one of the famous Triumvirate in power in Constantinople. He was Minister of Marine, and during the war, Commander of the Fourth Army Corps, operating in Syria and Mesopotamia. In the winter of 1914–15 he established his headquarters in Damascus for the campaign against Egypt. Less fearful of assassination, and hence less elusive than Enver, he was also more sociable and easy of access than was the Minister of War. I saw him many times and met him personally on several occasions, both in Syria and in Constantinople.

His physical presence was not imposing. His frame was powerful but stocky, but he had the most piercing glance I have ever met. Tricky and cruel as the man was known to be, he possessed a certain personal magnetism. Mr. Morgenthau likens him to a medieval robber-baron, and indeed the comparison is most apt. In his assumption of unlimited power, he reduced his subordinates to the state of serfs and abject retainers. He was virtually dictator in Syria, and the court of last resort, and he seldom concerned himself with his obligations to Constantinople. He could be relentless or generous as he pleased, but it is said of him generally that he was a man of his word, and that his promise once given was secure. He played the game of starving Syria with a mask of hypocritical regret, but his actions left no doubt as to his contempt and hostility toward the Arab race. It is also suspected that the concessions which he made to foreigners in his jurisdiction, especially in the American educational and relief-work, were made with the hope that, in case the campaign should go against him, and he should decide to cast himself into the hands of the Entente, these deeds would all be counted to him for righteousness. He was known to be bitterly anti-

German, and Francophile. He was also—to his credit
be it said—no friend of Enver or of the Beirût *Vāli*.

Partly through the innate cruelty of the man, and
partly through his consummate tactlessness, Jemal
Pasha succeeded early in the war in directing toward
himself the undying enmity of the Arabs. At the
time of the departure of the French Consul from
Beirût, at the outbreak of the war, certain extremely
dangerous documents were left in the French Consulate, hidden behind a false wall. When the American
Consul General, Mr. Hollis, took over the protection
of French interests in Syria, he implored the French
Consul to destroy any papers which, should they fall
into the hands of Turks, might serve to incriminate
Ottoman subjects. The French Consul, however, was
deaf to this appeal, and departed leaving behind him
numerous documents connected with the French propaganda in Syria. Some of these were signed letters
from Syrians with French sympathies promising financial and political support to any attempt France might
make to liberate the country from Turkish dominion.
These documents were undoubtedly evidence of high
treason on the part of those in the conspiracy, and
perhaps any government would have been justified in
dealing with the offenders as traitors. However, with
diplomacy and tact, the matter might have been handled in a way that would have increased rather than
destroyed the Ottoman prestige with the Arabs.
Jemal, as Military Governor of Syria, dealt with the
matter in a most summary fashion, and thereby roused
the revengeful hatred of the whole Arab race. Not

only did he hang without trial the principal offenders, whatever their rank or political following, but he so far overstepped the bounds of caution as to include in the number executed an Algerian prince.

It may be argued that during a time of war a government must resort to drastic measures to suppress treason, but the fact remains that the course which the Government followed was more disastrous than salutary in the long run. Moreover, previous to the war, the Arab party had been recognized by the Ottoman Cabinet, and the Sublime Porte had agreed to the existence of a decentralization party. It was not as though the Arab Nationalists had secretly sprung into being during a time of war, and had taken advantage of Turkey's preoccupation with military affairs to intrigue with foreign Powers. The result of Jemal's efforts to crush the Arab power was that thenceforward the Arabs transferred their allegiance to the British; and the bitterest enemies that Jemal Pasha had, both as a man and as a ruler, were those in the province under his administration.

The authority of Jemal Pasha in Syria was that of a military dictator, and in this capacity he frequently clashed with the civil authorities in the provinces under his jurisdiction. It has already been explained that the entire Turkish Empire was divided into states or *vilāyets,* under *Vālis,* or Governors, each of whom was directly responsible to the Sultan. The zone of the Fourth Army in Syria included three such *vilāyets,* Beirût, Damascus, and Aleppo. When the war broke out, the *Vāli* of Beirût was one Sami Bekir. He was a tall, florid Turk, who lived on fairly good terms with the foreigners. He frequented the so-called French Club, an organization which, after the breaking of relations, was *camouflaged* as the American Club (a complete misnomer), and still later as the Syrian Club. He was very fond of gambling, and owing to this passion, was on more or less familiar terms with a certain class of wealthy Syrians. His presence was always manifest in his goings and comings about the city, for he travelled in a large and very blatant yellow automobile. As he was not entirely in favour with the Young Turk party, and was also not above suspicion of having an itching palm, he was removed early in the war to Aleppo, and replaced by a man of an entirely different stamp.

Azmi Bey, the new *Vāli*, was then about forty-five years of age. He was slightly undersized, and gave the impression of physical weakness, which was further accentuated by his cruel and dissipated face. His black hair was slightly grizzled, as was his Van Dyck beard. In appearance he was more Armenian than pure Turkish in type, but in character he was a Turk of the Turks, and one of the very wickedest. He was openly known to be an agent of the Young Turk party, a tool of Enver, and one of that class of Turks who were fanatically anti-foreign. Nevertheless, his inordinate ambition frequently brought him into conflict with his party-leaders at the Capital, and there were at least two occasions when he was summoned to Constantinople and when his return to Syria seemed extremely doubtful. As former Prefect of Police at

Constantinople, he had a long record of crimes at his door, and it was known that on more than one occasion he had acted as political assassin, a convenient method of ridding himself of his enemies which he did not hesitate to employ in his later career in Syria. Azmi was the notorious cut-throat which the Young Turk party sent to Paris some time before the war to assassinate General Sherif Pasha, but on that occasion he bungled the affair and killed instead the Pasha's aide-de-camp. The deed was accomplished in broad daylight in the heart of Paris, and Azmi coolly descended from the scene of his crime to a waiting automobile, and was spirited away before the outraged French could apprehend him. Two years later at the instigation of his party he boarded a Russian steamer bound from Odessa to Egypt, which had called at Constantinople, enticed on shore another enemy of the Young Turk régime, whom he murdered that night in one of the dreadful dungeons of Stamboul. For his Paris crime the French Government offered a heavy bounty for him, dead or alive, should he ever enter France or fall into French hands. During the war his various villainies gained him such a reputation that he was in particularly bad odour with the Entente who ranked him with Talaat, Enver and Jemal in responsibility for the numerous atrocities which can be laid at the door of the party-leaders in Constantinople.

Like Jemal Pasha, with whom he was at swords' points—a fact which probably gained him the special favour of Enver—Azmi Bey was a man by instinct and actions eminently more suited to a barbaric rather than a civilized age. Although he enjoys the reputation of being somewhat of an ascetic, Azmi Bey was in reality profligate in his private life. A sister of charity gave me a circumstantial account of his attempt to abduct one of the orphans under her care, a tale which in no wise contradicts other reports that I have heard of his low moral standards. His chief virtues are said to have been punctuality, industry, and devotion to his official duties, even at the sacrifice of social pleasures. He was positively fanatical in his enthusiasm for Turkey, and there was nothing feigned in his hatred of foreigners, or in his resentment at their interference with Ottoman affairs. He was outspoken in his likes and dislikes, and made no secret of the fact that he lived in constant terror of assassination. He was never out of reach of a loaded revolver which he would have used in self-defence just as coolly as he had employed similar weapons for the destruction of his enemies.

On Azmi Bey and his minions rests the blame for most of the starvation and suffering in the vast district under his control. He was carrying out the extermination program instituted by the Young Turk Government, and in the execution of this congenial task he found great satisfaction also in venting his hatred against foreigners. He consistently either prohibited, or interfered with all relief-projects undertaken by the Americans in Beirût *Vilāyet*. He did countenance one or two relief-organizations carried on under the patronage of certain wealthy Syrians whose favour he wished to win for the financing of a large gambling casino and amusement park which he was building near the city. Incidentally, it is an interesting fact that this very casino, four months after Azmi's departure from Beirût, was being used by the British Army Y. M. C. A. He also established soup-kitchens which provided an erratic and insufficient food-allowance for a small fraction of the hungry of Beirût. At the same time, however, that he was nominally patronizing these, he was satisfying his vanity by wholesale attempts at city-improvement, which, however laudable at any other time, were the cause of injustice and suffering and were regarded by the people as merely another scheme of destruction on the part of the Government. Whole sections of the city were torn down to make new or wider roads. Property owners were not reimbursed for houses or shops thus destroyed, nor was any provision made for housing the hundreds of poor people formerly huddled in the crowded sections thus demolished. Men were forced to work on this roadmaking but were not adequately paid. While parts of the city were undeniably improved, other portions looked as if they had been destroyed by an earthquake. Nothing would convince a Jerusalem man who came to Beirût early in 1917 that there was no truth to the report prevalent in the Holy City that Beirût had three times been bombarded by Entente ships. Were not the evidences of it before him in what is now, in 1919, Allenby Street?

By 1917 Azmi Bey could not travel from his house to the city limits along the main thoroughfares without seeing in the streets all along the route people either dead or dying of starvation; yet he refused to let wheat into the city, and decreed that all foodstuffs should be subject to taxation or seizure at the border. Finally, when the Americans transferred their efforts at relief from the province under his jurisdiction to Lebanon, he attempted to put a stop to the work by deporting the two Americans who were especially active in the financing and the organization of relief-enterprises.

For more than three years Azmi Bey proved so useful an agent of the party of Union and Progress that he was suffered to remain in office, although there were times when his position seemed extremely precarious. As an official he placed his own interests above those of his country, and there is positive evidence of his corruption and abuse of his authority. He had the boldness to hint to Mr. Dana, three days before the latter's arrest and deportation, that there was trouble ahead which might be averted by the payment of $50,000. He was ultimately recalled in disgrace by the very party in Constantinople which had placed him in office, and was summoned to the Capital to defend himself against serious charges. The case went so badly with him that for a time he was imprisoned in the War Department; and shortly after Mr. Dana's release from his incarceration, when calling at the Prison one day, the Commandant of the Prison asked him whether he would enjoy the sight of his enemy behind the bars. His imprisonment was not of long duration, however, and he was soon strutting about the city as if he owned the place. On several occasions the Danas and I lunched at the table next to his at the Tokatlian Hotel in Pera, and I for one did not find that his presence whetted my appetite. Azmi Bey was one of that band of fugitives from justice who fled from Constantinople just before the British occupation. It is supposed that he sought sanctuary in Germany, where he is probably still hiding, although frequent reports of his suicide have been circulated in the Capital—probably with a view of terminating the extremely inconvenient interest which his enemies seem to take in his whereabouts. There are many who sincerely hope that he is still alive, and within the reach of retributive justice!

Muhhedin Bey, the Chief of Police in Beirût, proved an able and sympathetic assistant in any villainies which the *Vâli* devised. He was also a notorious assassin, and had been employed by the Young Turk party to murder the editor of the *Tannin*, whom he shot at noon on the Galata Bridge at Constantinople. Never was life in Beirût more precarious for Syrian or for foreigner alike than during the dual régime of these two men. No chief of police in Beirût ever had assembled about him such a number of unscrupulous private agents and cut-throats. He had any number of men on his spy list whom he could call into the office, hand a silver coin, and a slip of paper bearing the name of any individual whatsoever, and say, " I want that man killed." He could be sure that the task would be accomplished before another sun had set. His system of terror and extortion was unprecedented even in Syria. He formed false sugar companies, mining companies, and building companies, and sent the bogus stock certificates through the town, where by forced sales among the merchants he collected a splendid private fortune.

In the summer of 1916 Muhhedin Bey was sent to the wheat region about Urfa, in Mesopotamia, to purchase wheat for the needs of Beirût *Vilāyet*. Had he fulfilled this mission honourably, there would have been no more popular man in the whole of Syria. He would have been worshipped as a national saviour. However, being a Turkish official, he saw in this merely an opportunity for lining his own pockets. Out of several hundred carloads of wheat purchased by him with public funds only six ever reached Beirût! Shortly after his return to Syria, he pled urgent personal business which necessitated his going to Constantinople for a flying trip. He had only just passed Aleppo when agents of Azmi, who was exasperated at the failure of his colleague to divide the profits, overtook him and searched his baggage. Among the boxes which were said to contain merely his personal effects and gifts of silk and wool for friends in Constantinople were found some £tq. 16,000 in gold which he had intended to send to Switzerland by his aide, to be there invested for him. He was brought back under guard to 'Aleih where he was put through that famous Court Martial which has unjustly condemned so many Syrians to death. He was acquitted! What subsequently happened is more or less a matter of gossip; but it is said that in an interview with Azmi Bey, the latter handed Muhhedin Bey a revolver with the hint that there was no room on earth for such a scoundrel as he. The disgraced Muhhedin went first to the Police Headquarters with the intention of murdering his successor, Hakki Bey, whom he suspected of having assisted in his humiliation; but, the acting chief being absent, he returned to his house. A few moments later the guard at the door heard a revolver-shot, and entering the apartment found Muhhedin dying. His body was buried as criminals are buried in a shallow grave in the sands outside the city. When the news of the event reached Constantinople, Talaat (?), a connection of his by marriage, raised a terrible commotion; and the body was disinterred and was sent in state to the Capital. Never was a man's decease occasion for greater rejoicing! Many an innocent person slept more easily the night after his death was publicly known. His successor, Mukhtar Bey, was a quiet, friendly Turk who tried to soften conditions as much as he dared under the reign of Azmi, and who had a splendid record for fair dealing. In comparison with that of Muhhedin, his régime seemed positively beneficent.

It is indeed refreshing, after the rehearsal of the infamies of such men as Azmi and Muhhedin, involving as it does the memory of many episodes connected with my uncle's experiences so terrible that even the thought of them makes me shudder, to turn to two other Turks who ruled in Syria, but who were men of entirely different spirit. One was Ali Munif Bey, for two years Governor of the independent province of Lebanon. He was, of course, affiliated with the Young Turk party, but he was a man of quiet force, who by the dignity of his character and his diplomacy succeeded in maintaining friendly relations with the powers in Constantinople without surrendering himself to them as a tool. I have already described his attitude in regard to the relief-work which he wished the Americans to transfer from Beirût to Lebanon, and I believe it is fair to say that under him Lebanon enjoyed comparative justice and tolerance in affairs connected with governmental administration. During his régime poverty, starvation, and suffering were not in the least abated; but the amelioration of those conditions depended on matters entirely beyond the control of the Lebanon Governor. It has already been pointed out that Lebanon was not self-supporting, and that the wheat-supply must be imported from regions lying to the east and northeast. Even the beneficent governor in the " island " of Lebanon was powerless to alleviate the suffering of his subjects, without the support and coöperation of the governors of these wheat districts, and of the land that lay between. Against the hostility of Jemal Pasha and of Azmi Bey, and their determination to brook no interference with their plan of starvation, especially in Lebanon, Ali Munif was impotent.

Early in 1917 he was called to Constantinople to occupy a position in the Turkish Cabinet, and was given the portfolio of Minister of Public Works and Public Instruction. To my mind, his conduct after the Armistice is the best possible commentary on his character. When Enver, Talaat, and Jemal fled for their lives from the approach of the Entente, Ali Munif Bey was one of the very few men who had held office under the Young Turks' régime who was not afraid to face the incoming armies. He remained quietly in Constantinople; and although he was subjected to an interrogation, I am told that he was granted honourable acquittal. As far as I know, he still resides in the Capital.

His successor as Governor of Lebanon, Ismail Hakki Bey, who had formerly held the position of Turkish Counsellor in Egypt, was a humane and obliging man, interested in the welfare of his people, and an open promoter of education, sanitation, philanthropy, and public welfare. He was firm in administering justice, and was not afraid to renovate his own administration by the imprisonment of certain officials whose habits had become rather lax under former administrations. He recognized the defects of his own government, and did not hesitate to call upon foreigners for ideas and for assistance whenever progressive action could be taken wisely. When Azmi Bey was called to Constantinople, Ismail Hakki's jurisdiction was extended over Beirût also, and he held the joint office of *Vāli* of Beirût and *Mutaṣcrrif* of Lebanon. He remained in office until a few days before the arrival of the British on October 8, 1918, when he hurriedly departed for Constantinople. He left behind him a record for clean and honourable dealing, and all who knew him are frank to admit that during his régime the country prospered as it had at no other time during the war.

There are two other public characters connected with affairs in Syria who should rightfully be included in this chapter of personalities. One is Tahsin Bey,

Governor of Damascus, and the other is Bedri Bey,
Governor of Aleppo. Tahsin Bey's character was far
superior to that of any of his associates; and had he
been Governor of Beirût, the history of life there during the war would have been far different from what it
was. I believe that Tahsin Bey of Damascus can be
identified with Tahsin Pasha who was Governor of
Van just previous to the Armenian massacres in 1915,
but who was replaced by Jevdet Bey, because he could
not be relied on to carry out the government policy of
persecuting the Christians. Tahsin Bey was a hard-
working, forceful man, and a born politician. He cor-
dially hated the Germans, and opposed them point by
point in their repeated attempts to take over the administration of Damascus. Had the *Vāli* there been
a less positive character, the Germans would undoubtedly have succeeded in establishing a Teutonic administration in that great Oriental city, which they realized
would be a priceless possession for supplies and for
equipment in any project which they might undertake.
If they had carried out their plans, they would most
certainly have precipitated an Arab revolution in Damascus and in the surrounding region, with the probable result that Syria would have passed under British
control many months earlier than this actually happened. Tahsin Bey was openly friendly to American
relief-work; and once, while visiting Dr. Dray's hospice and soup-kitchen in Brummâna, as the guest of
Ismail Hakki Bey, he was so impressed with the work
that he gave an order for one hundred and fifty tons
of wheat.

Bedri Bey in Aleppo was likewise a prominent figure in Constantinople politics. At the outbreak of the war he was Prefect of Police in the Capital, but was later given the post in Aleppo, probably in order that he might extract his share of the financial plums in Syria. While in Aleppo he instituted great plans for civic improvement, and thereby accumulated large sums of money which went into his private pocket.

These are the men who caused the public sorrow of Syria; and I wonder whether the reader will pause in his reading, as I have done so often in writing, to marvel that such men could live and rule during the twentieth century. Could anything equal the characters of Azmi and Jemal as a proof of the real nature of the Turkish Government, and could anything be surer evidence that Turkey as a nation has forfeited all rights to an independent existence? Such men as I have just described are not exceptional, but are typical Turks; and a country which can produce, and which tolerates such men as its governing class, cannot be trusted with the safety of subject-races.

X

THE EFFECT IN SYRIA OF AMERICA'S ENTRANCE INTO THE WAR

ALL our special excitements in Beirût seemed to come on Sunday, we could never understand exactly why, although some ingenious member of the community suggested that it was because Sunday was to the Moslems what Tuesday is to us. On Saturday, corresponding to our Monday, the officials, back at their desks with that fresh zeal for work which attends the opening of a new week, turned over their records, and recalled to mind items which had perhaps been overlooked in the pressure of more urgent affairs. Sunday, like our Tuesday, was the day for executing any newly formed resolutions. Moreover, Sunday was the day when we were known to be at home, or in church, and when, therefore, we were easy to find. Whatever the reason may have been, the fact remains that Sunday was the one day in the week when we were particularly liable to annoyance from the Government.

The day when the severance of diplomatic relations between the United States and Turkey was announced in Beirût proved no exception to the general rule. On April 22nd, one of the first hot days of early summer, as we were coming out of church, we noticed a policeman stationed at the outer gate of the Press, which is adjacent to the church. Had I been asked to state anything extraordinary about the appearance of the street at that time I should probably have overlooked the policeman, for the gray uniform of the Turkish police was too familiar a sight to attract notice. But to the manager of the Press that motionless guard meant something out of the common. Later in the day, when we learned of the breaking of relations between our own country and the Ottoman Empire, the presence of that Turkish guard became instantly intelligible. The average Turkish official saw no distinction between the rupture of diplomatic relations and an actual declaration of war. Thenceforth Americans also were regarded as belligerents. The policeman at the gate was the first step in Turkey's plan of confiscating American property, just as she had seized the property of other belligerents.

The three days that followed were full of excitement. A rupture between America and Turkey came as no surprise; indeed, we had believed for months that it was imminent, so that when the blow fell, we were not found wholly unprepared. Against just such an emergency the manager of the Press had removed to other quarters certain valuable papers and money, including a small reserve of gold. No attempt was made to open the Press on Monday morning. No attention was paid to the Turkish guard, and he remained at his post quite oblivious of the fact that the manager and certain employees had entered by a back door, and were working inside the shuttered building transport-

ing records and valuables to a place of safety. These
were carried to a private house in the Mission compound, at that time unoccupied, the owners being in
America. In the course of the morning enough had
been removed to relieve considerably the anxiety of the
manager who anticipated that the next move on the part
of the Government would be to seize the Press building
and confiscate everything it contained. Great as the
loss would be if they should appropriate the paper and
other printing supplies, especially the thousand precious electroplates for the Arabic Bible (each one
worth $12.50), that loss would be insignificant in com-
parison with the taking of the contents of the safe:
deeds, records, accounts, and cash.

After this transfer had been successfully completed,
Mr. and Mrs. Dana and I went to the American Consulate to see what we could do about removing the gold
that was stored in the Press safe there. Here likewise
there were Turkish police stationed at every door, but
they made no attempt to interfere with our entering.
We knew, however, that they might insist on searching
us as we came out, for other Americans had already
been subjected to that indignity earlier in the morning.
This being the probability, how were we to remove that
gold? There were $40,000, wrapped in rolls of about
$200 each. Mr. Dana dared not carry any himself.
It was out of the question to think of loading it into a
satchel and boldly walking out with it. Finally we
decided that Mrs. Dana and I should make several trips
between the Consulate and our house, about a mile
away, each time carrying as many rolls of gold as we

could stow away inside of our clothing. One by one, the rolls were dropped down our necks until the weight was as much as we could carry. We found that we could manage about $6,500 apiece at a time, and in three trips we succeeded in removing the entire amount without arousing any suspicion on the part of the guards. The gold was subsequently packed in a tin box, and was plastered up under a marble floor in our house until such time as conditions in the country would once more permit of its circulation. Every one anticipated that the time would come when Turkish paper-currency would be entirely discredited, and then lucky the man who had a little " hard cash "!

On May 7, 1917, the American Consul General, Mr. Hollis, the Vice-Consul, Mr. Chesbrough, and one of the American clerks, Mr. Wadsworth, left Beirût for the overland trip to Constantinople. The Dutch Consul General in Beirût was entrusted with American and Allied interests. In Aleppo these gentlemen were joined by the consular representatives from Aleppo and Damascus; but owing to delays *en route,* they reached Constantinople just a few hours too late to leave the Capital on the Ambassador's train. With customary malice, the Porte hindered their departure from the Empire as long as possible, and I believe it was July before they were allowed to leave by the Balkan Express for Europe.

On Monday, April 23rd, the American Press did not open its doors. This was the first time in half a century that the Press had been closed on any day other than a holiday. For two months guards were stationed at the gate of the Press, and at the entrance of the Mission compound. Finally the Chief of Police called Mr. Dana to interview him and requested him to open the doors and resume business, stating that the closing of such an important commercial house was creating a very bad impression in the town, considering the great work which the Press had done. The truth was that the Syrians were so indignant over the affair that the Turks realized how thoroughly they had roused public sentiment against them by this particular act.

Mr. Dana refused to open the Press so long as the premises were under police guard, and demanded official explanations as to why the guards should be kept there. The Chief replied, " You know that we are about to go to war with your country." To this Mr. Dana answered, " It is not so. Your Government and my Government are not on speaking terms because you are an ally of Germany with whom we are at war, but that does not give you the least right to interfere with the private property of Americans."

Finding that cajolery had no effect, the Chief then resorted to the favourite Turkish ruse of threats. " If you don't open the Press," he stormed, " I will seize it and confiscate everything in it." " Yes, I know you can do that," the manager replied quietly. " You have the power and no one can stop you. I have no fear of anything that you or any other Turk can do. My only fear is that a blot may fall on the good name of the Press through anything I myself may do. The Press has operated in this country under Turkish rule for nearly one hundred years, and never in all that time has its good reputation been tarnished. I have no terror of you or of the worst you can do. I should be afraid, however, to meet my board of directors in the United States, if I had brought discredit upon the institution entrusted to my care. I should be doing that very thing if I were to accede to your unjust demands. What you take by force does not shame us. What I voluntarily surrender to you does."

A silence followed this defiant speech; then with the unaccountable caprice of the Turk, the Chief of Police reached for his telephone and gave orders that the guards should immediately be removed from the Press and the Mission property. Mr. Dana thanked him without comment. The next morning the doors of the Press were again opened.

As a matter of fact, much of the Press's work had, during this period, been carried on from the unofficial quarters in the private house previously mentioned, although publicly the Press had ceased to function.

After the breaking of relations, the greatest problem with which the Press had to contend was the matter of the Syrian remittances. It was no longer possible to pay these as they had formerly been paid, for the Ottoman Government, which made no distinction between an actual declaration of war and the mere rupture of diplomatic relations, would have branded the continued attempt of the Americans to make payments to Syrians as enemy propaganda, with serious results not only for the Americans, but also for the Syrian beneficiaries. At this juncture a German stepped into the breach, proving by his tolerance and philanthropy that he was one of those rare individuals, and rarer Germans, who were blessed with a larger vision, and a love of humanity greater than their devotion to the Prussian system. This German was Mr. Ernst Schoemann, Director of the *Deutsche Palästina Bank*, and Swedish Consular Agent in Beirût. No higher tribute could have been paid to him than the attitude of the American community at the time when there was uncertainty as to whether the American interests should be entrusted to the Dutch or to the Swedish representatives in Beirût. In Constantinople, the American interests in Turkey had formally been handed over to the Swedish Minister, the Honourable C. d'Anckerswaerd, although the Swedish home-government and its Constantinople representatives were admittedly pro-German. In Beirût, however, where the Swedish Consular Agent was in fact a German, but was in reality infinitely less fanatically Prussian than his chief in Constantinople, the Swedish representative was rejected, and the American affairs were entrusted to the Dutch Consulate General. The American residents as a whole had been united in their desire that Mr. Schoemann should be placed in charge of their interests, so great was their confidence in him, and so warm their admiration. There was nothing of the Hun in this quiet gentleman, and it was impossible to associate him with the deeds of his countrymen in Europe. Indeed, in his rare comments upon the course of military events, he frankly deplored the brutal spirit of Prussian militarism. To the very last, namely, until his departure in September, 1918, before the British advance, Mr. Schoemann lived in most cordial relations with the Anglo-American community of Beirût.   Indeed, the American Press owes it to him that it was able after the breaking of relations to continue certain of its payments under Azmi's very eye. It was only Mr. Schoemann's willingness to coöperate in these relief-payments to Syrians which prevented a complete cessation of this line of work, and a consequent increased mortality in Syria during the winter of 1917–18.

At the moment of the rupture, there were many lists of Syrian remittances already in the Press in the course of preparation for payment.   When the Press was closed, there was no way in which to effect the delivery of the designated amounts; and daily the policemen at the gate turned away scores of people who had already been instructed to call for their money.   It seemed wicked to consider returning these amounts to New York with the bare statement that it was no longer possible to continue this relief-work. It would have been like snatching a loaf of bread from a starving man whose fingers had already closed upon it.   Consequently, Mr. Dana arranged to have these payments made at the *Deutsche Palästina Bank* as though they were a part of the Bank's own transactions.   All during the summer of 1917 the remittances to Syrians were continued by this method, but the necessary funds were raised by the Press through the sale of checks on its New York bankers, a risky method, since a Turkish military restriction forbade the negotiation of foreign checks.   These, however, were antedated, and therefore, bearing no evidence that they were not issued previously to the publication of the ban, could be circulated without any legal penalty.

The experience of the American Press after the breaking of relations may be regarded as fairly typical. The American Mission representatives did not suffer any greater inconveniences, although they needed to be constantly on the alert to save their property from the rapacious Turks. The American Mission Hospital in Tripoli, and the private residence of William S. Nelson in Ḥomṣ were the only American properties actually seized, and these were not taken until several months after the breaking of relations.

The Syrian Protestant College fared no worse, although it was known that the Germans were doing their utmost to use the Turks as their catspaw in appropriating this most desirable site in Beirût. A German meteorologist actually went up to the College and announced his intention of taking charge of the observatory, and settling his own family in one of the faculty homes. It was largely due to the enmity between Jemal Pasha and the Germans that the College was allowed to continue. Had Jemal Pasha himself wished the premises, he would not have delayed an instant in seizing them, but he preferred to leave the Americans in possession, if by so doing he could spite the Germans. It is known, however, that Jemal had promised a special favourite of his, one Hallidé Hanum, a Turkish Mme. de Staël, that, when he was ready to turn the Americans out, he would make her directress of education in Syria, and give her the College site into the bargain. The time for this move not being ripe, however, he was pleased to play the part of College patron, and even assisted in securing supplies of foodstuffs during two years when the institution would otherwise have had to choose between closing or assuming an enormous financial obligation.

XI

HYSTERICAL AND HISTORICAL
EXCITEMENTS

L IFE for foreigners behind the curtain in Syria
was never free from strain. They would be
ashamed to refer to the lack of customary
luxuries as a hardship, for in that respect they were
no worse off than every one else throughout the world.
Their sympathies were constantly harrowed by the
sufferings of the Syrians, but there was no country in
Europe where they could have escaped such vicarious
pain. The whole atmosphere was charged with excitement. There was an unbroken chain of events
which served to keep the nervous in a ferment of unrest. Some of these occurrences stirred the Ottoman
population, and through them acted on the foreigners,
while others concerned only the foreigners themselves.
Even if there were a lull for about two weeks, the
monotony was sure to be broken, and it seemed as
though nearly every six months something really
momentous occurred. We became accustomed to the
state of unrest, and those who were great-minded
learned to live calmly, and without undue anxiety for
the future.

Those were days which tried the souls of men. Each
was thrown back upon himself, and many a philoso-

pher, or a Christian, was forced to redetermine just how much his beliefs were really worth. Did he have faith? If so, was it strong enough to fortify him in such trials? Did he truly believe that he was " bigger than anything which could happen " to him, and that he need concern himself with only one day at a time? or was his creed merely a jumble of meaningless phrases which proved of no value in the face of a real crisis?

The problems of those days were not the phantoms of hysteria which could be routed by strength of will. They were not passing anxieties, or inconsequential perplexities, but were the very problems of life and death. Some one has compared our predicament to that of a band of miners trapped in a subterranean clamber with every exit blocked. In such a catastrophe there is nothing that the victims can do to save themselves. They must wait for rescue from without; and they know to a certainty that, if help is long-delayed, it will come too late.

As the years of the war dragged out, the problems which confronted us grew increasingly grave. We faced our situation humorously at the beginning, in the confidence that such abnormal conditions could not continue many months. We branded Kitchener, with his three-year plans, as a pessimist of the darkest dye, and we felt that we were remarkably forehanded if we bought anything with an eye to the future. Theoretically we all believed in preparedness, but no one had any idea what to prepare for. The war had no parallel in our previous experience. The longest night must end, and the sleepless watcher welcomes each passing hour in the knowledge that it brings the dawn just so much nearer. But the continued duration of the war brought no promise of its conclusion. " It might be for years; and it might be forever." We knew only that, if we hoped to endure to the end, we must provide for years ahead. My uncle's advice to us sounded like the Chess Queen's promise to Alice of " jam to-morrow "—a to-morrow which was always one day ahead. " Buy for three years," he told my aunt and me, and he repeated the advice when the war was three years old. It was all very well to say that, but the question was: How much did one really need of everything? We had never bought in quantity before. Those of us who had always made retail purchases according to immediate need had no idea how many pairs of stockings, how many handkerchiefs, how much soap, tooth-paste, or writing paper we used in a year. Even those who thought that they were able to estimate fairly accurately failed to reckon on the inferiority of wartime articles. Where a tooth-brush had lasted two months before, it might not stand one month's service now. How many American housekeepers before the war knew how many gallons of molasses they would use *annually*, if there were no sugar; how many quarts of dried beans; how much cooking fat; how much baking-powder? And yet housekeepers in Syria had to learn these things by bitter experience.

The first flurry after the outbreak of the war was financial. The Anglo-American community felt the pinch almost as acutely as the Syrians, for few of them had ever before experienced such a sudden cessation of income, and they simply could not comprehend it. They had money in the bank. Why could they not draw it as usual? Scenes which occurred in the offices of the College and the Mission Treasurers were both pathetic and ludicrous, and members of the American community begged, literally begged, in vain for a pound or two. The shortage occurred also at a particularly awkward time, in August and September, when most people wished to buy supplies for the winter. This year, in view of war uncertainties, every one was especially desirous of laying in an ample stock of provisions.

The acute financial shortage lasted only a few weeks, but during the whole of the conflict we were not entirely free from distress in this regard. Most families felt the necessity of securing and concealing, with great difficulty, a little gold to use in any emergency, such as a complete collapse of the paper-currency, deportation, or an enemy occupation. During the second year of the war, when gold was outlawed and Turkish paper substituted, prices took a sudden flight. They had been steadily increasing ever since the outbreak of hostilities, but with the introduction of paper-currency their rise was phenomenal and wholly disproportionate. The purchasing value of Turkish paper dropped as low as one-sixth that of actual coin, or "hard" money. This, coupled with the rise in prices, made living expenses enormous, and it took no little courage to face the steadily increasing figures in the account-books. Of course, this financial strain was not peculiar to Syria, but the distinctive features here were four: the popular lack of faith in the Ottoman paper-currency issues, the inability of the Government to cope with speculation in currency values, government connivance at the cornering of necessary foodstuffs, and the subsequent famine prices of certain necessities. For those who care to read them we have appended at the end of the book a few figures illustrating the almost incredible rise in prices.

Even before the Entente Powers broke relations with Turkey, we felt the first slight results of the combat. A German ship, the *Peter Rikmers,* carrying ammunition, rubber, and other miscellaneous freight, sought refuge in the port of Beirût. Her cargo was unloaded as quickly as possible, and not a day too soon, for a Russian cruiser came strolling along the coast, caught the *Peter Rikmers* as she was trying to escape from the harbour, and sank her then and there. Not many days later the same cruiser carried off from the harbour a small coast steamer, and a launch called *La Syrie.* The ownership of the latter was American, but it was apparent that the Russians supposed it to belong to a Turkish subject who might use it in naval warfare against the Entente. After these incidents the local authorities scuttled all small craft along the coast for two reasons: to spite the enemy, and to remove temptation from any Ottoman subjects who might so far shirk their patriotic duties as to try to escape by sea.

Within a few months after the beginning of the war,

the Turkish campaign against Egypt was in progress, and later the British counter-campaign against Palestine. We experienced practically nothing in the way of actual warfare, but we were reminded of military events in numerous amusing and inconvenient ways. The Government commandeered all the large bags that it could lay hands on, and even assessed every Ottoman household with a specified number. In order to comply with this military requisition and to avoid trouble people were forced to use their window-curtains, their couch-covers and even their extra clothing to make bags. It was a fortunate thing for the country that the Government was satisfied with empty bags! The Turks had had an inspiration. They were going to use sandbags in the Egyptian campaign. They also appropriated for army use another very important household article, the indispensable oil-tin; and in time these empty cans, because of their scarcity, were valued at more than their original pre-war cost when filled with the best Standard Oil!

Visitations from enemy warships were fairly frequent during the first part of the war and, like the later and less frequent visits, were sometimes accompanied with excitements. It was a popular fallacy to expect an attack from the coast and a bombardment of Beirût, although it was technically an unfortified town. There were lively recollections of what was called "the Italian bombardment of 1911," and the psychological effect of the appearance of a cruiser on the horizon was amusing to watch. Naturally the uneducated people, especially the Moslems, supposed that an English or a French attacking force would conduct itself just as victorious Turks would do; and they imagined that the entry of the enemy would be attended with violence, massacre and bondage. Furthermore, the attitude of the Turkish garrison in Beirût did not tend to inspire confidence either in the conduct of the enemy, or of their own prowess. Most of these troops were quartered in the barracks, a large building on a hill near the American compound, but they had also a good hiding-place in a pine-grove at the edge of the city. Like the famous " King of France, who had ten thousand men; he marched them up the hill, and marched them down again," the officers in charge of these Turkish soldiers always gave them " movement orders " whenever a cruiser was sighted; and they were hurried, bag and baggage, from the barracks into their place of concealment and safety outside of the town. During some weeks they were kept very busy moving back and forth.

Not only did the troops occupy themselves with hiding whenever a cruiser appeared, but many of the civil population made preparations for a hasty departure. It was not an uncommon sight to see porters hurrying through the streets with bed-bundles, or even less portable articles such as wardrobes, and large mirrors. A goodly number of people, especially Moslems, left Beirût for Damascus, which, being well in the interior, was generally considered a safer place. Some of these emigrants returned after the first excitement and worry were past, but many remained throughout the war. Such was the popular alarm at

anything which in the least resembled a warship that on
one occasion the Collier *Vulcan* that came with coal
for the U. S. S. *North Carolina* caused great con-
sternation. The *Vulcan* presented an array of der-
ricks which was most alarming and unusual. We
were just returning from an afternoon drive when
this formidable craft arrived, and our coachman suggested the advisability of our at once fleeing the city.
I can still see the relief in his face when we explained
that it was merely an American ship bringing coal for
the cruiser.

It was not uncommon for the visiting war-craft to
deliver messages whose purport was either published
or leaked out. On one occasion the Beirût authorities
were reminded that any attempt to build trenches or
otherwise fortify the town would open the door to
enemy attacks. In spite of this, trenches were dug all
along the sea road, guns were placed in a monastery on
the sands which commanded the only landing beach
near the city, and the hills back of Beirût were trenched,
covered with barbed wire entanglements, and equipped
with gun emplacements. For a long time the Entente
cruisers limited their action to sinking small sailing
craft which, though warned against so doing, were
smuggling wheat from one port to another along the
coast. Another not unusual proceeding was for the
French ships to attempt the destruction of important
bridges on the highway along the sea. The one near
Tripoli which carried the Tripoli-Ḥomṣ railroad was
an especial object of attack. The Turks retaliated for
these hostile acts by erasing the French inscription at

the entrance of the Dog River Pass which com-
memorated the triumph of the army of Napoleon III.
These petty bombardments and spasmodic demonstrations did not accomplish much more than to keep the
Turkish forces in northern Syria and the Syrian
populace in a constant state of perturbation. Even
excitement palls eventually, however, and the country
became so habituated to the existing state of affairs
that people almost gave up hoping for a real occupation.

When German submarines began to use various
points on the Syrian coast as their bases, the vigilance
of the coast-patrol was redoubled. Then we saw fewer
large ships and more submarine chasers. These made
constant calls on Jûneh, a small town northeast of
Beirût, which was known to contain a good deal of
petroleum. A Russian cruiser had, earlier in the war,
destroyed the Standard Oil depot there, but it was believed apparently that there were other petroleum
stores in the town. We watched several spectacular
bombardments of this little place.

One day a trawler came hurrying along as though
seeking for something near Beirût. A German submarine was then in port, and some of her crew were
on shore. Without waiting for these men, she dived.
The trawler, however, feigned ignorance of her presence, and went on south where she gave information
to a British destroyer. That night the submarine came
back to get the rest of her crew and more supplies.
Early the next morning, Sunday, we were startled by
sounds of heavy firing near the port, and presently a

shrieking shell passed fairly low over our house. Two more shells followed, and more sounds of firing at the port. The British destroyer had arrived bright and early in hopes of surprising the submarine. She passed by the harbour entrance and headed toward Jûneh, but suddenly turned and boldly steamed straight into the port which was supposed to be heavily mined. The submarine was not quick enough to escape and was wounded, although it was impossible at the time to tell how seriously. When in her course around the harbour the destroyer came near the shore, Turkish soldiers on guard at the Ottoman and German banks tried a little sharp-shooting at the men on her deck. Her reply was several shells fired over the city as a warning to the inhabitants to keep under cover, and then she turned her guns on the two banks which quartered these rash soldiers. Banking business in Beirût was suspended for the next ten days, while idle stone-masons and plasterers enjoyed an unusual run of business. After having settled her score, the destroyer departed, apparently satisfied with her morning's work. A few days later we heard from a reliable source that a local photographer had been asked to photograph for identification the bodies of several German submarine sailors washed ashore near the city.

I doubt whether such events caused as much stir as the terrible distant naval battle which some of our friends once viewed from the mountains. It was about sunset and a dozen or more ships were seen in deadly combat off toward the dim horizon in the west.

The firing of the heavy guns could be heard distinctly. Skeptics insisted that it was all imagination, but the witnesses would not be convinced. Surely they had lived in Syria too long to mistake the combination of a native wedding, celebrated by rifle-fire, and the fanciful shapes of evening clouds at sunset for a naval battle!

It is not to be denied that many who lived in Syria during the war were upset merely because they let their imaginations run away with them. Most of these argued that there could be no smoke without fire, and that there must be some foundation for certain persistently recurring reports. One of these was that Beirût, as well as other coast cities, might be evacuated, or at least that the foreign residents might be required at very short notice to move away from the seaboard. While there seemed little likelihood that this would really happen, one could scarcely avoid giving the matter some slight consideration as a possibility. The evacuation scare reached its height in the summer of 1917, after we received in Beirût various tales of the occurrences in Jaffa where the larger part of the population was ruthlessly harried out without conveyance, and was driven into the interior. As the lack of vehicles was as serious in Beirût as at Jaffa, I know one American family which made a little push-cart, ostensibly for use in transporting its goods to the mountains, which also would save the children many weary steps in case they were expelled from the city and had to travel on foot.

Another fear which caused perhaps more uneasi-

ness than evacuation, was deportation. Many of us
had this brought very near home by the exile of a number of our belligerent and Syrian friends. With such
incidents constantly occurring, it is not surprising
that some families kept bags always ready, packed
with the necessities for a journey; although it must be
admitted that, except in a very few instances, people
who were ordered to leave had plenty of time to gather
together whatever they needed for their change of residence. After the deportation of Dr. Stewart of
Latakia, Dr. Nelson of Tripoli, and Mr. Dana of
Beirût had proved conclusively that not even Americans were exempt from this form of persecution,
those who believed in preparedness felt themselves
wholly in the right. This explains and largely justi-
fies certain suggestions made by the Syrian Protestant
College to its American faculty in December, 1917.
Besides giving numerous useful hints as to the settlement of any business matters, destruction of papers,
disposal of valuables in case of need, and as to clothing, food and medicines for a journey, the list suggested also having handy Turkish-French visiting
cards and a copy of Jemal Pasha's speech in which he
claimed to be friendly to the College. The contents
of the list of suggestions is of less importance, however, than the fact of its existence, which was illus-
trative of what one might call the state of mind of the
times.

It would be trite to suggest that Syria was scourged
by the "Four Horsemen of the Apocalypse." That
simile has already been overworked in other connec-

tions. But we were not the only community which found fresh interest in our Bibles, as we recognized the striking similarity between the conditions in Biblical days, and those of our own war period. For a time we were able to describe our situation to friends at home by referring them to certain Scriptural passages, but eventually this device was discovered in the post office. _ The Mohammedan censor, in order to'hold his job, became a devout student of the Bible, and he waged such war against Bible allusions that he even held up letters which suggested necessary corrections in the proof of the new Arabic Reference Bible.

We used our concordances to good advantage when we wished to describe the terrible plague of locusts which swept over the land in 1915. The description of Pharaoh's seventh scourge might have been written in April, 1915: "And when it was morning, the east wind brought the locusts. And the locusts went up all over the land, . . . and rested in all the coasts; . . . very grievous were they . . . for they covered the face of the whole earth, so that the land was darkened; and they did eat every herb of the land, and all the fruit of the trees; . . . and there remained not any green thing in the trees, or in the herbs of the field through all the land . . ." (Ex. 10.)

I was driving down to Sidon when the first swarm of locusts appeared, and the sight was far more awful and impressive in the open country with its free sweep of sky than it was in the city. The sun was suddenly darkened, and looking up we saw that the air was full of whirling winged forms. The effect was strikingly similar to a driving snow-storm, only in this case the mammoth flakes were yellow and black. They settled as softly as snow on field and tree, and when they again took flight they left the land utterly devastated. They had devoured every leaf and flower and fruit. In some cases they had even stripped off the bark. The ground where they had rested was bare of every living plant. More awful still, they were carnivorous. There were numerous instances where mothers left their little children alone at home while they went to the fields, and returning found little more than the skeletons, clothing and flesh having been devoured by these horrible creatures. The swarm would settle for several days in a locality, and then sweep on leaving in its wake ruin and destruction. Five or six times during that summer fresh hordes descended upon us. Always the first warning of their approach was the din of tin pans, beaten by anxious land-owners in the vain hope of frightening away the insects before they settled. Not only did they destroy that year's crops, but in many localities they permanently injured the trees by their repeated onslaughts. Such a plague had not been seen in Syria for more than forty years; and, coming as it did on top of all the hardships of war-time, it convinced the people of the wrath of the Lord. Man had done his worst for the country, and now nature had turned cruel.

The one thing above all others which most piqued the Turks was the realization that everything which went on in the country was known abroad as soon as it happened. One morning in

August, 1915, fourteen political offenders were hanged
in Beirût, and the Alexandria and Paris papers
of that same day published the names of those executed. This is only one striking instance of the ef-
fectiveness of the Entente intelligence service. There
was quite evidently constant signalling from the mountains to cruisers out at sea, and the Turks were at
great pains to discover a wireless station which somehow was keeping the enemy posted. The College was
subject to annoyance on several occasions while search
was made for an imaginary wireless outfit. When I
recollect two mere boys who were held for months in
the military prison in Constantinople on account of a
toy wireless, pronounced by German experts quite un-
usable, it makes me· shudder to think what misinter-
pretation might have been put on the most innocuous
piece of laboratory apparatus in the College. Even
the observatory dome was never opened during the
war lest the astronomer be accused of communicating
with the enemy. On one occasion one of the College
community was requested to take down the signals
flying in her yard in sight of the sea. In vain she
protested it was merely the usual weekly wash. No,
they were signals to the enemy's ships, and down they
must come!

Another cause of worry to the local government was
lights in the houses. The majority of the Beirût
houses have high arched windows opening on balconies
facing the sea. Foreign residents especially were required to darken their windows when the lights were
on. This was no small item of expense when the

size of the windows was only equalled by the cost of the cloth necessary to cover them. On several occasions a policeman came to request us to darken one of our kitchen windows which we found especially hard to reach. Our domestic would request the policeman to close it for us from outside by the delicate manipulation of a broom handle, and after a few calls with similar results the policeman found it more convenient to overlook that lighted square.

It was just like the Turks, however, to fret over such unimportant matters and to overlook the truly significant things that were going on under their very eyes. Spies were constantly coming and going between Syria and Egypt, and it is surprising how many people in Syria were in their confidence. Fishermen along the coast carried on a lucrative, if somewhat risky, trade in facilitating escapes by taking people on dark nights out to patrolling enemy vessels. One night the French head of a large commercial concern disappeared with his entire household, including the dog. Their unfinished supper was left on the table. No one knew what had become of them, but the instance conjured up visions of a sudden chance to escape on a French cruiser. Such events as this reminded us that the atmosphere in which we lived did not lack melodramatic features.

There were times when some of us almost wished that a cruiser would call with orders from our Government to whisk us off. Travel for even short distances was made as difficult as possible. One could not even cross the Beirût border for a picnic without giving an account of oneself. The Turk was always so suspicious that he made himself a tremendous amount of unnecessary trouble. Frequently travellers between Beirût *Vilâyet* and Lebanon were subjected to as thorough a search as though leaving Constantinople for Europe. On one occasion an American was detained at the border because the Turks discovered among his papers a map his children were sending to their grandmother in town. It was a sketch of a favourite swimming-hole, but even such fanciful names as " Fairy Dell " and " Giant Cave " struck the Turks as highly suspicious. The Turk certainly does not have much imagination!

In order to go to the mountains for the summer one had to have a *vesika,* or travel-permit, besides permission to transport in either direction foodstuffs and personal belongings. Any one not fully in the good graces of the Government had to wait a long time to obtain his papers. Sometimes the officials saw other possibilities in the matter of *vesikas,* as when in 1915 the Chief of Police, Muhhedin Bey, intimated to Mr. Dana that he might have his permission to take his family to the mountains if he would pay the small fee of $1,000. Needless to say, we stayed in Beirût that summer! By the following year Muhhedin Bey had removed himself as an obstacle to any one's obtaining a travel permit.

If the Turks would only apply their genius in proper directions they might accomplish wonders. I doubt whether any race can equal them in malicious ingenuity. They are past masters at devising annoyances, and no ogre ever surpassed a Turk in the capacity for inventing barbaric forms of torture, or in enjoying the discomfort of his victims.   In May, 1915, the Government achieved a regular *tour de force* which resulted in the arrest of practically the entire American Mission.   In May and December the Mission held in Beirût its semi-annual meetings.   It was a custom of many years' standing and the Government had never thought of objecting to the gathering which was known to concern itself solely with Mission problems.   On this occasion the meeting was held in the accustomed place, a large room in one of the houses in the American Compound.   Suddenly the police appeared and arrested the whole company.   When the elders and dignitaries of the Mission were haled before the Chief of Police, they were told that they had been arrested for violating a law which the Turks meant soon to publish.   The Americans should have known that very shortly any kind of gathering would be illegal.   Of course, the Government had no case against them, but it succeeded in causing much inconvenience and annoyance.   That being the case, the Turks could afford to be magnanimous, and in about two hours they released their prisoners, first taking pains to escort to the city limits all the out-of-town missionaries.

A little piece of malice like this, however, generally cleared the atmosphere, for the Turks were usually so pleased with themselves that they were quite genial for some time afterwards.

In that same summer of 1915 we were all much distressed by the difficulties which befell certain Americans who had come down from Armenia. Among others who had come to Beirût in the hope of leaving by sea were Dr. Floyd Smith and his family from Diârbekr, and Mr. Harrison Maynard and his family from Bitlis. Dr. Smith had been expelled from Diârbekr because of his interest in the Armenians, and both he and Mr. Maynard were known to have been witnesses of recent Armenian atrocities. Both were imprisoned and taken before the 'Aleih Court Martial for trial. Dr. Smith's trial was only half finished when he was sent down to Beirût to await sentence. A mistake in the police office gave him a loophole for escape. Within an hour he and his family were safe on board a vessel in the harbour, while the Turks frantically searched for their lost criminal. It must have infuriated them that within a few months Dr. Smith was back in Armenia, behind the Russian lines.

Mr. Maynard was detained several days in 'Aleih and probably only the facts that the American cruiser *Tennessee* delayed sailing three days, and that she was known to be waiting for him, effected his acquittal in time for him to board the ship.

It was a rather homesick day for some of us when we bade farewell to the *Tennessee* as she steamed away from Beirût with her long home pennant streaming behind, and her band playing " Home, Sweet Home." It seemed the last chance for any of us to leave Syria, save by the dreaded overland trip to Constantinople. There were later opportunities to leave by cruiser, but most of these were limited to American

Jews, although there were other Americans who were most anxious to obtain permission to go, many of whom had come from the far interior with the hope of finding in Beirût some opportunity to sail.

The worst of the annual typhus epidemics occurred in the winter of 1916. Not only was the death-rate highest that year, but the disease attacked a number of our best Syrian friends, as well as members of the American community. The way in which different persons were affected by the fever was pathetically indicative of their interests. One brave little nurse exclaimed: " I am glad I have it, for now I can nurse typhus cases without further fear, and with knowledge of the disease from personal experience." Another sweet lady was most concerned during her delirium concerning the poor whom she had been visiting; and because she was under the delusion that she had robbed her own family to share with the starving Syrians. The American Vice-Consul evidently had the Jews on his mind. He was terribly distressed because he thought that he had allowed some of them to leave by cruiser without proper passports, and the nurse would catch him getting out of bed to write telegrams on the subject to the American Consul at Alexandria. While we could smile at such vagaries when we knew the patients were on the road to recovery, we had to fight down our horror of the disease; and although we never let the idea interfere with our daily pursuits, we often wondered: who next?

No survey of our trials during the war would be complete without some reference to the domestic problems. As elsewhere in the world these played a part in the general stress. I regret to say that before the close of the war scarcely any gathering of women could take place without sooner or later the question of food becoming the uppermost topic in the conversation. The cost of living and the food question were two demons always lurking in the background. During the winter of 1916 the Government set a limit to the quantity of supplies that one might have on hand. It was rumoured that houses would be searched and that superfluous stores would be confiscated. Such a procedure on the part of the conscienceless Turkish police was appalling. Most people acted on faith that this was merely a threat, although they deemed it safer not to keep all their provisions in one place. One American lady told me recently of her dread lest her family of children should not have all they needed to eat. Late one night she hid wheat and other supplies in an ancient Phœnician well which, in the course of some repairs, had been discovered under her house, and the opening of which had been thoughtfully *camouflaged* in case of future need. The same well was used to conceal some family silver, glass and other valuables. This is only one of many cases where personal property was hidden. Syrians gave their valuables into the hands of Americans, and Americans placed theirs in the care of Syrian friends. No one could judge which would be the safer place in the final outcome. Even members of our own family concealed some things in our attic so well that we had difficulty afterwards in finding them!

All this is amusing to look back upon after a lapse of time and when the strain is past. As a matter of fact, we were not nearly so uncomfortable in some respects as our friends in America imagined. All through the whole time of difficulty there was among the Americans a spirit of hopefulness and optimism regarding the ultimate course of events which mitigated every passing trouble.

XII

1917—THE YEAR OF HORROR

W E have previously spoken of life in Turkey during the World-War as life behind a curtain, but it would really be more accurate to describe it as life in a house of many chambers. We lived for a while in one room; and when that became no longer habitable, we progressed to another, the very existence of which, perhaps, we had not suspected. When we were ejected from this room and the door closed behind us, we stood for a moment bewildered in the passageway; and then, conquering the fear lest we might be entering a veritable Bluebeard's chamber of horrors, we tried another closed portal; and if it yielded, crossed the threshold. This was especially true in the matter of relief-work.

At the outbreak of the war, the Americans in Syria attempted to render relief through the tried and tested channels of the Red Cross Society. For a while they were successful, but at the end of a year, the Beirût Government forced them to abandon this form of activity; and the work, in a slightly modified form, was transferred to Lebanon. When the Armenian and Syrian Relief Committee in America took over the financing of relief in this portion of the Near East, and the Christmas Ship of 1916 was expected, the

entire energies of the Beirût Relief Committee were
concentrated on arranging for the best possible dis-
position of this precious cargo. The definite announcement that the ship had been deflected preceded
by only a few weeks the declaration of war between
the United States and Germany, and the rupture of
America's diplomatic relations with Turkey. The
American loss of neutral status provided the Ottoman
Government with a long-sought excuse for definitely
and positively prohibiting any foreign interference in
internal affairs, even in connection with relief matters.
At the end of April, 1917, when relations between
America and Turkey were broken, the Beirût Relief
Committee had only $140,000 in its treasury, and this
sum was used secretly through Syrian agents. When
this was expended, and it was no longer possible, on
account of the closing of mail and telegraphic communications with America, to secure further funds
from home committees, the Beirût Committee dis-
solved, and thus permanently terminated its relief
activities.

The only remaining source of income from the outside world was, therefore, the Syrian remittances
through the American Mission Press; and these were
continued in spite of government opposition, and the
avowed determination of the Ottoman authorities to
deal drastically with any individual, foreigner or native, who should be discovered in the act of communicating with the enemies of the Turkish Government, in
which category the United States was now included.
The charitable organizations of America were not

discouraged, however, in their efforts to relieve this afflicted country, and the Presbyterian Board of Foreign Missions arranged with the Enemy Trade Board of the United States to issue Trade Licenses for the amounts available for Syria. In view of the fact that postal communications with the Ottoman Empire had been completely suspended, the State Department agreed to forward the weekly lists from the New York Treasurer by official courier from Washington to Switzerland or Stockholm, and thence to Constantinople. From Constantinople onward the lists were concealed between packets of paper-money, and were mailed as such to Syria in sealed and insured envelopes. It took some months, however, to evolve this system of communication; and even when it was established, what had formerly been a river of income dwindled to a mere trickle. Delays were inevitable, and the necessity for absolute disguise of the source of these remittances, combined with the problem of securing cash, made this work both dangerous and difficult. It was, nevertheless, continued without interruption up to the moment of the British occupation of the country in the autumn of 1918, in spite of the fact that Mr. Dana, who had originated the system, was deported, and was forced to leave before he could even see his successor and explain to him certain details of which no one but himself was cognizant.

When the Beirût Relief Committee ceased to operate, the American Mission determined to assume full responsibility for the continuance of the relief-work thus abandoned. They held a secret meeting at one of the mountain villages in a region where so many of the Americans were summering that a gathering of others from outlying districts would pass unnoticed by the Government. In that meeting they voted to expend the sum of $250,000 on faith that when communications with the supporting committees should eventually be reëstablished, the Armenian and Syrian Relief Committee would reimburse the Mission Board in New York for the amounts advanced by the Syria Mission. In lieu of positive assurance that the committees at home would in reality make good such disbursements, the members of the American Mission in Syria agreed to assume personal and individual responsibility to the Mission Board in America for this advance on faith.

When the Syria Mission learned beyond a doubt that the *Cæsar* was not coming to the coast of Syria, they felt convinced that the cargo would be sold, and the proceeds of the sale turned back to the home-committee. It was imperative to obtain from America assurance that these funds were in reality held there at the disposal of the Syria Committee. If that proved to be the case, the Mission would be able to borrow money locally to continue the work. The difficulty of obtaining such information was due to the hostility of the Turks which made it inadvisable to send through regular channels any written message giving evidence of the continued activity of Americans along relief lines. The cablegram had to be so worded that if intercepted *en route* it would not be comprehensible to the Turks. A fertile brain, therefore, devised the following cryptogram, and a special messenger was sent with it to Holland: "Calpurnia's husband (referring to the *Cæsar*) unable to make delivery. Can you duplicate amount your cable twenty ($100,000), enabling make purchases locally pending reaping (Stop). Reply, using only this cable number (37)."

The scrap of paper containing the precious message on which depended the lives of so many thousands in Syria was safely smuggled through the repeated examinations in Turkey to which every traveller was subjected, through Bulgaria, Austria, and Germany; but it was discovered and confiscated on the German border just as the messenger was about to enter Holland. He had, however, memorized the words of the cable which he dispatched from the Hague. In five weeks the reply, forwarded through Sweden, reached the Treasurer of the Syria Mission in Beirût. Just the two words, "Thirty-seven granted," but what a world of hope they represented!

There must have been a leak *en route* somewhere, because, three weeks after the departure of the messenger and only a short time before the arrival of the answer, Mr. Dana was arrested and taken to the police station, where he was asked who "Calpurnia" was, and what was the meaning of the word "reaping." His reply convinced the Turks that Calpurnia was a humble person pining for her absent husband, and that "reaping" meant only a certain season of the year.

Other single grants for relief were also reported by the Mission Board in New York in cryptic cable messages through Switzerland or Stockholm. One of them read " Fifteen thousand morerel committee mercy." These funds were administered by the Treasurer of the Syria Mission, and represented virtually a continuance of the former Red Cross work.

In January, 1918, when Mr. Dana reached Constantinople, he discovered that the Armenian and Syrian Relief Committee had appropriated an amount of $50,000 monthly, beginning on July 1, 1917, for relief in Syria, part of which was available in Switzerland. This regular allowance was continued as long as the war lasted, although after the British occupation, first the Red Cross, and then the American Committee for Relief in the Near East was responsible for the amount.

The program first followed in distribution was that previously instituted by the Red Cross, and accordingly appropriations were made to all the out-stations. This was in response to the appeals of individual missionaries from villages in itinerating districts, or of resident foreigners, consular officers, *etc.* The burning desire of every one who had the welfare of Syria at heart was to organize a big relief-work and carry it on as such; but the hostility of the Turks, bent on their scheme of exterminating the Syrians, made this impossible. Whatever relief was given by the Americans themselves had to be done under the guise of carrying on their regular mission work. They laid in foodstuffs for relief distribution under the pretence of buying supplies for the schools, native helpers, and their own Mission community. Only the stupidity of the Turks in not realizing that fifty tons of wheat was a superabundant supply for fifty or one hundred children in a Mission school made such purchases possible. Where there was no possible cloak of mission activity to disguise the real motive of relief, it was impossible for the Americans to appear in connection with the work, and the plan adopted was to place sums for relief disbursement in the hands of any thoroughly reliable person who was in a position to render aid in districts where the need was greatest, and where there was no danger of overlapping. These agents were preferably Syrians, but in some cases they were foreigners, for example, a Swedish lady living in Lebanon, and a German sister of charity.

Special and definite instructions always accompanied these grants, as to the plan of relief to be followed, and the classes of persons to be helped The appropriations were usually delivered monthly, and the agent was required to give each time a report on his methods, the classes of beneficiaries, and all details connected with the efficacy of the assistance rendered. It is unfortunate that these reports were necessarily all verbal, as it results in placing the full burden of financial responsibility on the shoulders of one man, the Mission Treasurer. However, the risk of written evidence of relief activities was so great that no one would have ventured to sign his name to a statement which, if it fell into the hands of the Turks, would incriminate not only himself, but the Americans from whom he had received the funds, and the Syrians to whom he had distributed them.

Such assistance as has just been described usually

took the form of supplying destitute families with a regular allowance either of funds or of food, according to conditions of prices, accessibility of food-supply, *etc.* In a district where wheat was purchasable in the open market it simplified matters for the relief-agent to distribute cash. In other localities, where food-stuffs had to be imported from a great distance, and with endless difficulty in the matter of permits and transport, it was necessary to distribute the actual food commodities. Money would have been useless. Indeed, in some cases the people were able to pay for supplies furnished by the relief-agents, but wholly unable to obtain provisions for themselves, even with money in hand.

A very effective form of relief was the distribution of wool, which was given out to women to spin and to knit into garments, some of which were kept for the family of the worker, others being turned back to the wool distribution center. These were subsequently sold for the benefit of the relief-work, or were sent to orphanages or to soup-kitchens where they were distributed to people in desperate need of clothing.

The form of relief-work that the Mission, perhaps, most favoured was the assuming of a fixed responsibility for a number of orphans. There were thousands of children bereft of one or both of their parents who would surely die if they were not provided with shelter, food and clothing by some charitable organization. The fundamental principle of selection in American relief-work throughout the war was the attempt to choose individuals with a view to their prospective value to the country. By this test the care of the children was, obviously, of paramount importance. About six or seven thousand orphans were adopted by the Mission, and were cared for in large orphanages, in shelters, or in private families which were willing to accept the care of an orphan in exchange for their own support by relief-funds. In many cases the little waifs were fostered by mothers who had already several children of their own, but who considered the addition of another five or ten to the family only a slight additional burden. Among the lower classes in Syria the care of a child is at best a rather haphazard affair, and the parents consider that they are amply discharging their duty, if they provide him with the same food that they themselves eat, with one or two indispensable articles of clothing (not always those that we consider indispensable), and with a bed to sleep on. Instruction in personal hygiene, or in moral cleanliness, schooling, or medical care are deemed quite superfluous; and the child is alternately indulged and brutally flogged until he grows strong enough to defend himself against corporal punishment. From that day onward he is independent. It will be seen, therefore, that the care of an orphan is not such a responsible matter as it would be with us; and if the child is given three meals a day, the responsibility whether he lives or dies is not the parents' or guardians', but the Lord's.

It was found more generally satisfactory to gather the orphans into hospices and care for them *en masse*, especially since these hospices were frequently operated in connection with a soup-kitchen, thus minimizing the expenditures of both. Children who had parents or guardians, and a shelter for the night were merely provided with nutritious food twice a day, and perhaps, with certain articles of clothing. It was only those who were absolutely friendless and destitute that were taken into the shelters.

In a country that has been ravaged by disease and starvation with all their attendant ills, it is not sufficient to feed and clothe the body, but provision must also be made for proper medical treatment. I have heard a person who lived in Syria during the whole period of the war state his belief that very few people in Syria actually died of starvation, but rather of disease. In one sense this is partially true, but it leaves out of account the fact that most of the malignant diseases prevalent in the country were the result of famine conditions and malnutrition. Philanthropy, therefore, to be of permanent value must be carried on in conjunction with a medical campaign. The doctors and nurses deserve an ample share in the credit for what was accomplished in Syria for the welfare of the people. Indeed, the relief-work may be likened in organization to a modern army, in which the medical and sanitation departments are no less important than the transport service and the commissariat. In addition to the support of doctors and nurses in connection with the soup-kitchens and orphanages, regular appropriations were made from the relief-funds to hospitals, or to independent practitioners and nurses who were limited in their possibilities of usefulness by the inability of the average patient to pay fees for medical services or hospital care. Funds were also made available in local pharmacies for the free distribution of medicines and drugs according to doctors' prescriptions, and charity beds were maintained in several hospitals. It must not be supposed, however, that this line of activity freed either the physicians or the hospitals from their own charitable responsibilities. On the contrary, it was only a means of widening the scope of their activities. They had themselves assumed more than their full share of philanthropic obligations, but the need was greater than they could cope with unaided. As a matter of fact, many a patient was turned away from a hospital, even when he had friends who were willing to guarantee his expenses, merely because there was no possible way of making room for him.

The most painful of all the responsibilities laid upon the handful of Americans in charge of the relief-work was the necessity of selecting from a vast number those who should constitute the small group that could be supported by the limited funds at the disposal of the Mission. It seemed that they were usurping a divine prerogative when they deliberately determinated that of two individuals who applied for assistance one should be taken and the other left. It was literally the old case of the two women grinding at the mill. In general, however, an honest attempt was made to predict the probable permanent value of an individual to his country, and where the choice lay between the young and the aged, the well-educated and the illiterate, the breadwinner of a family and the independent individual, in almost every case the former was chosen. The resulting necessity of refusing many who had every claim on our sympathy was a heart-breaking ordeal, but one from which there was no escape. The first principle of economy was to keep alive those on whom funds had already been expended, and the second was so to distribute further funds as to accomplish the greatest good. Whether the Mission succeeded or failed it is perhaps too early to judge. It must be a satisfaction, however, to the American public to know that the funds they contributed carried fully 150,000 Syrians through to the end of the war, each one of whom would indubitably have perished had not America's generosity furnished the means of salvation. Tens of thousands more were saved before they reached the limit of utter destitution.

The fatalism of the East is proverbial, and has both its good and its evil effects on the Oriental. This fatalism, exaggerated during the war to positive apathy by the overwhelming sense of helplessness and impotence, generated a pitiful spirit in the people. There is a tendency on the part of the Syrian to accept all the events of life, whether good or ill, as dispensations of Providence, and the death of a child, or success in a business venture are alike accepted as "min-Allâh" (from God). At times one rather deplores this implicit faith, which often robs an individual of the stimulating sense of personal responsibility for his success in life. There is more incentive to keen living in our English adage, "God helps those who help themselves." However, in Syria during the war, I think that even the Americans were at times oppressed with this sense of impotence. Every possible obstacle blocked the pathway of life, and even the most conscientious efforts to help oneself and others, and thereby merit the assistance of God, seemed fruitless, so long as the powers of evil had the upper hand. The struggle on the part of the Syrian people to exist, over against the determination of the Turks to exterminate them, seemed to me like the futile effort of a nation to build some tremendous edifice. Stone by stone the pile was erected, but as fast as the workers built the Turks destroyed. The most that any one could do to assist in the unequal competition was to help the builders replace on the foundations the stones that were being thrown off by the despoiler. In this case the race was to the swift. To-day circumstances are far different. The building is now growing, and there is scarcely a hand that is hindering. The Turk has been ejected from the land, and Europe and America have joined forces with the Syrians to aid them in their endeavour to fashion for themselves a place among the nations of the world.

Pessimism is not the word with which to describe this peculiar mental attitude among the less intelligent classes of Syrians. Fatalism comes nearer the truth, and yet is not exactly descriptive of that strange indifference, amounting almost to impersonality with which the masses regarded the future. I recall particularly one instance which has remained vividly in my memory. I had determined to walk from the

Lebanon village of 'Aleih where I was summering in 1917 to 'Abeih, some ten miles further along the same mountain ridge. There were no carriages or pack-animals for hire and I was perplexed as to how I should transport my suitcase, which such a tenderfoot as I found too great a burden. Through servants' gossip it became known in 'Aleih that I was to make the excursion, and the circumstances under which I was travelling, and the evening before I left 'Aleih a neighbour woman came to the house and begged for the privilege of carrying my bag for me. At first I demurred, for I could not allow another woman to carry a load which I myself could not manage. However, she insisted that she was strong, and being a mountain woman had been accustomed to carrying much heavier loads for greater distances. Moreover, she was in desperate need of money, work was scarce, and she was eager to avail herself of any opportunity to turn an honest penny. Finally I consented, and we set out together the following morning. We walked slowly, for the heat was intense even in mid-October, and the suitcase, while not very heavy, hindered my companion's progress. As she knew a little English, having served as a domestic in one of the community families, we fell to chatting; and before our walk was over I had learned another of the pitiful tales which almost daily reached our ears. Her husband had emigrated to Brazil some years before the war, leaving her with three children, and no means of support except the funds which he sent home. With the war, his remittances had stopped, and she did not know

whether he was alive or dead. After she had told me
simply, and without the least note of complaint, of the
terrible struggle she had to keep the wolf from the
door, she asked me how long I thought the war would
continue. Naturally, I knew little more about it than
she did, but I had not the heart to give her too discouraging an answer. "Perhaps we can live through
this coming winter, for the Americans have helped me
a little, and I am receiving some assistance from one
of my brothers who has a little shop; but if it does not
finish by a year from now, I and my three children will
surely die." I tried to speak hopefully to her, but I
knew only too well that her words were quite true.
And her case was one of thousands—perhaps even less
serious than that of others, for she was receiving " a
little assistance," and most of the others had no aid
at all.

As I have just said, all the best American efforts at
relief were merely preventive, rather than curative.
We had put our shoulder to the wheel, as the figure
goes; but push as we might, we could accomplish no
more than to keep the cart from sliding downhill again.
We could not make it advance by even one revolution
of the wheel; and indeed it seemed as if even our
restraining efforts were fruitless, and that the time
must come when the cart would plunge down upon us,
bearing us with it to destruction. The Turks, moreover, were doing their utmost to push it backwards.
Thousands of dollars of American money had been
poured into Syria, and had accomplished a vast amount
of good, but further tens of thousands must follow,

else all that had already been expended would be wasted. The situation would have been difficult enough from the relief standpoint had there been merely the economic forces to contend with, but with the Turk doing his utmost to undo everything that could be done for relief, directly blocking every move in advance, and persecuting either Syrian or foreigner engaged in the work of assistance it was well-nigh desperate.

The winter of 1916–17 was the worst that I myself experienced in Syria, although I believe that the following year, when I was in Constantinople, was even more ghastly. Disease and starvation spread abroad throughout the land. In the city, refugees from Lebanon, driven down to the coast by the hope of there obtaining work, or at least of escaping from the bitter winter of the mountains, died in the streets. There were days when on the walk of a mile from our house to the office, Mr. Dana and I would pass as many as ten or twelve people either dead or dying by the roadside; or with death only a few hours distant. During the winter typhus raged, and in the summer cholera, dysentery, and pernicious malaria swept over the whole country. One passed four or five funerals each day on any route, and the same coffin did service for every corpse in a district until it literally fell to pieces. In Lebanon conditions were even more distressing. In the larger towns like 'Aleih, the dead were gathered off from the streets in the morning, and were thrown out on the hillside back of the town, where at night the jackals and hyenas found them. In more isolated villages, especially in the high barren regions of North

Lebanon, the whole population perished of starvation and disease. There are certain hamlets where the living population was completely obliterated, and where to-day many of the houses still contain the unburied skeletons of their former occupants.

The Government made no effort to ameliorate conditions, although for a time it kept up the pretence of rationing out flour to the poorest inhabitants of each Lebanon village. I happen to know that during the summer of 1916, when this particular hypocrisy was being most widely advertised, in a village near Shweir, in August the monthly rations were three months overdue; and even for the month of May, in which a distribution had been made, no one had received his full allotment. This pretence of Government assistance was sustained largely by those who found this means of robbery one of the most fruitful ways of preying upon the unfortunate people. It also had an element of zest, for it kept the poor in a state of constant hope without giving them enough to preserve life. It was the gossip of 'Aleih that same summer that Jemal Pasha had sent a carload of wheat as a present to the poor of that village, and that it had been seized by a wealthy Moslem in the town and sold for his own profit. I cannot vouch for the truth of this story, but I do know that it is typical of what actually occurred. The bread which the Government distributed in most cases contained no wheat at all, but was an unwholesome mixture of barley, corn, millet, and even earth and tares. Certain diseases resulting from malnutrition, such as pelagra, hitherto practically unknown in

Syria, became increasingly prevalent, and the germs of scabies, dysentery, typhoid and malaria were everywhere. It was more than heart could bear to travel about in Lebanon, and see the terrible evidences of famine and death that stared one in the face. The foreigner was literally besieged with requests for help, which he could not grant; and the wretched people who had besought him turned away with the dumb pain of a wounded animal, but never a word of complaint. To give to one beggar in the street meant that twenty would spring up out of the ground to demand alms; and all of us had incurred special responsibilities, such as the entire support of as many individuals as our means would permit, so that we could not scatter our funds to give one loaf of bread each to a hundred people, when a hundred loaves would keep one person alive for more than a month.

The most surprising thing to me in the whole situation was the absence of organized lawlessness, or even of consistent raiding. I have frequently stood on some mountain ridge and looked across the canyon to a similar spur on the opposite side. From that bird's-eye view I have marked the remote and tiny hamlets, the isolated clusters of houses, even the single buildings standing quite apart; and have wondered why in such a country robber bands had not sprung into existence. There are fastnesses in Lebanon, both secret and impregnable, where from ten to a hundred desperate men might make their lair. Thence they could sally forth to raid and terrorize, and no power of law and order could have restrained them. There were, of course, certain districts where brigandage was not uncommon, and there were numerous cases where men were robbed and murdered for their real or fancied wealth. But such instances were the exception; in general, life and property were respected, and it was quite safe even for an individual to travel about in the mountains.

The traces of those terrible years are still evident in Lebanon, and there are villages which to-day are deserted and in which the houses are falling into decay. The history of the average Lebanon family during the four years of the war was somewhat as follows. The breadwinner was either a day-labourer or the possessor of a small piece of land which he had inherited from his father and his grandfather, and which annually afforded him a scanty yield. Perhaps his land was planted with mulberry trees. If so, the first crop of leaves was fed to the silkworms during the spring, and the later crops furnished fodder for a cow, or served to fatten a sheep which was killed and salted down for the winter. Perhaps he had a truck-garden, whose meagre crops were only sufficient to feed him and his family of six. In any event, he lived a hand-to-mouth existence. He had nothing laid aside for a rainy day; and when the war came and the silk industry ceased, and he had no money with which to buy seeds for his garden, he had no alternative but to sell his land, except the piece on which the house stood, trusting either that he might find work in the city, or that the war might end, and conditions immediately, as he ignorantly supposed, resume their normal course. He failed, however, to find work, and the second year of the war commenced. Then he sold everything in his house except the beds on which his family slept, and the one or two indispensable cooking utensils. Later, he attempted to sell the house; but failing in this, he stripped the tiles from the roof, and sold those, and finally the iron or wooden beams that supported the roof. He and his family moved down into what they call in Syria a *ḳubbeh,* or vaulted cellar on the ground level. This tided him through the second year of the war. Typhus, which was raging in the village, carried off his wife and one child during the winter that followed. Of the four motherless children that remained the eldest, a girl of ten, became the housekeeper, if such a term can be applied to the woman in an establishment which possessed neither furniture, utensils, nor a house that was intact. The baby died of dysentery, and the father of cholera during the summer of 1916. The three other children were driven to begging, and two of them died of starvation and exposure. The sole survivor of that family, a little boy of five, was found at the point of death by Dr. Dray, the English doctor in charge of the orphanage and hospice at Brummâna, and was nursed back to life and health. About that Brummâna work I want to tell you next.

XIII

HOW AN ENGLISHMAN KEPT FOUR THOU-
SAND SYRIANS ALIVE

THE Brummâna Hospice is even more widely
known as " Dr. Dray's Relief Work," for it
was originated and maintained through the
efforts of Dr. Arthur Dray, a member of the Faculty
of the Syrian Protestant College and head of the
Dental Department.   Dr. Dray spent most of his early
life in Syria; and although he was an Englishman,
took his medical training in the United States.   After
completing his extensive education, he gave up the
great career that lay before him in America to return
to Syria, where he believed that he might be of even
greater service.   Not only is he preëminently *the* dental surgeon in the whole of the former Turkish Empire, but he is also licensed to practise in several other
departments of the medical profession.   His special
interest, however, is in his dental work, and in the pur-
suit of this passion he has brought untold blessing to
Syria.   There are comparatively few countries in the
world to-day that can compete with America in the
science of dentistry; but thanks to Dr. Dray, and his
associates and pupils of the Dental School of the

Syrian Protestant College, Syria may soon rightfully boast that she has more skilled dentists in proportion to her population than many countries more advanced in other ways.

Dr. Dray's position in Turkey during the war was unique. He had won the respect and confidence of the two most influential Turks in Syria, largely through their gratitude for his professional services; and although he was an Englishman, and therefore an enemy, he was privileged above any other foreigner in the country. The Turk is not celebrated for his honesty, his patriotism, or his philanthropy, and his instinct is to punish with the utmost cruelty any one who possesses these qualities. He does, however, recognize an honest and fearless man, and respects him, when once he has satisfied himself that these qualities are inherent and are not to be overcome by intimidation or cruelty. There is much of the animal in the Turkish nature. Figuratively speaking, a bold and steady gaze will make him cringe, but the least sign of fear will arouse his brute instincts and his thirst for blood.

Dr. Dray was one of the trio of British doctors on the Faculty of the Syrian Protestant College who were deported with their fellow-countrymen in December, 1914, but who later were allowed to return to Beirût in order that the Medical School of the American College might continue to produce doctors who could, upon graduation, be drafted into the army. One midnight in the summer of 1915 Dr. Dray was visited by Turkish police who presented orders from Jemal Pasha commanding him to proceed immediately to Jerusalem.

The police would furnish no explanation of this peremptory order, but Dr. Dray's natural assumption was that the intent was hostile. It was something of a relief, however, to be told that he must bring his surgical equipment.

That night he travelled to Damascus, and upon his arrival there he was told that in an hour or two there would be a special train to take him on to Jerusalem— a special train for a belligerent doctor, when the German Commander-in-Chief was practically the only personage in Syria who travelled in such style! Even Jemal Pasha himself preferred less conspicuous modes of conveyance. Arrived in Jerusalem, Dr. Dray was conducted immediately to Jemal Pasha's quarters in the German *Stiftung* on the Mount of Olives, where he was required to operate without a moment's delay on an influential Turkish guest of Jemal Pasha. The Pasha and his companion, who was a member of the royal family at the Capital, had been driving together when a shot was fired into their carriage. It had evidently been intended for the Commander of the Turkish Army, but it hit the other man, inflicting serious facial injuries. The wound had been neglected, and the patient was in a very grave state when Dr. Dray first saw him. The operation proved miraculously successful, and Jemal Pasha was delighted. He showered the doctor with attentions, and returned him to Beirût with a letter of highest recommendation to the Governor of that city. He dropped the warning, however, that if he ever had cause to suspect that the matter had gotten out through Dr. Dray, it would go hard with him. It was evident that the Turk was determined that no hint of the unpopularity which had resulted in an attempt on his life should reach his jealous colleagues in Constantinople. Needless to say, Dr. Dray guarded the secret as his own, and never mentioned it to any one until after the British occupation of Syria, and the flight of the Pasha from Constantinople. The great Turk's gratitude reminds one of the story of Androcles and the Lion. Thenceforth he could not do too much for Dr. Dray, and there were even times when the Doctor was forced to remind his " grateful patient" that he was himself a British patriot, and therefore an enemy of the Turk. Even this defiance, however, only seemed to increase the Pasha's respect, and as long as he was in power he manifested consistent friendliness to the Doctor, and through him to the College.

The letter of recommendation brought by Dr. Dray from Jemal Pasha to Azmi Bey was not at all favourably received by the latter, and it was not until he himself was suffering from an ulcerated tooth that he too surrendered to necessity and sent for Dr. Dray. From that time onward he was very friendly toward the Doctor, and on several occasions even commanded him to dinner. Those must have been pleasant meals, for although the Governor entertained his guest graciously, he took no pains to hide the loaded revolvers which were to be found in every part of his house always within reach of the notorious assassin!

All this is by way of explanation how it came about that a year later Dr. Dray, an enemy of the Turkish régime, but the friend of the Syrian people, was permitted to organize and carry on extensive relief-work in Lebanon. He had chosen for his summer-residence the village of Brummâna, about fifteen miles from Beirût, one of the few summering places accessible from the city at that time when transport was unobtainable, and one had to depend upon one's own legs to carry one up and down the mountain. It so happened that Jemal Pasha was also summering in Brummâna; and although Dr. Dray encountered him seldom, it later proved a fortunate thing for the poor in a great district that these two men visited in that locality at the same time.

Dr. and Mrs. Dray were guests at the Saalmüller Hotel, which is delightfully situated on a ridge commanding one of the loveliest views of Lebanon, Beirût and the coastal plain to the north and west, and the ascending steeps of the higher Lebanon ranges to the south and east. By reason of its pines, in a region where trees are all too few, Brummâna had become a special favourite among the nearer summering places; and had it not been for the distress about them, Dr. and Mrs. Dray would have enjoyed a most restful and peaceful vacation. Apart from the habitations of men, with the ever-lovely panorama of Lebanon scenery to delight and refresh the soul, Swinburne's lines came to mind:

> " Here, where the world is quiet,
>   Here, where all trouble seems
>   Dead winds' and spent waves' riot,
>   In doubtful dreams of dreams."

From the eyrie of Lebanon the war seemed incredible, and trouble only a " doubtful dream of dreams "; but into such a reverie of peace the spectre of reality never failed to penetrate. The solitary dreamer was startled by a whine at his elbow, " God has been generous to *you*, oh my brother! " The very personification of misery met the lifted eye. A walking skeleton clad in filthy rags extended its claw-like hand.

The first morning in Brummâna, the Doctor took his book out under the trees, but he was followed by several persons who, having learned of his arrival, had come to him for help, even as the multitudes besieged that other Healer when He went out from the city into the hills. Dr. Dray did not dismiss them, but encouraged them to tell him of their need; and after they had gone away, he sat for a long time and pondered. Here was evidently an opportunity to heal and save, but before the work could be undertaken there was still the problem to solve: shall I feed them to-day and let them starve to-morrow, or shall I use my limited means to care for a few individuals for an indefinite period, until the end of the war, or until they can become self-supporting? Never was there a greater test of faith than the decision which resulted from that morning's reflection. Dr. Dray determined to accept a limited number of protégés whom he promised himself to support until the time of need should be past. He saw his way clear for some months to come, but how he should fulfil this self-imposed obligation in the uncertain future he left for the future to answer.

Jemal Pasha's presence in the village rendered the

work that Dr. Dray contemplated quite impossible until the former could be induced to give his sanction to such a charitable undertaking. On an appropriate occasion the Doctor sketched briefly the tragic conditions that obtained, and intimated his readiness to do what he could in the way of relief. The Pasha graciously gave his consent on condition that no males between twelve and sixty should benefit by the enterprise; but he brusquely stated that, if Dr. Dray ever quoted him as having made that stipulation, the work would immediately be terminated, and the Doctor punished for his indiscretion.

The necessity of excluding men from among the possible beneficiaries of such work as Dr. Dray planned was a matter of little importance. It was the pitiful plight of the women and children—particularly the children—that made his heart ache; and to the men who later solicited his assistance he replied that they should by rights be serving in the army of their country, and that he could do nothing to countenance the neglect of patriotic duties. Later the Pasha dropped a remark which was interpreted as permission to employ a few men as labourers, but the number of the men on the list of beneficiaries was always negligible.

In the beginning, Dr. Dray adopted the plan of giving to those few whose need he had investigated and found to be genuine small amounts of money, only sufficient for their daily needs. In a few days, however, large numbers who had heard of this relief thronged to the hotel, and Dr. Dray realized that he must, in fairness to the other guests, make other arrangements for his relief-work. Accordingly, he arranged with a woman in the village to prepare a simple meal of cooked vegetables and bread for the fifteen persons whom he had accepted as his protégés. This experiment, however, did not prove a success; but a Syrian friend, Mrs. Cortass, offered her services for the preparation of the one meal a day which Dr. Dray had decided to give those he was helping. Fifteen partook of that first meal, but by the end of a year the Brummâna Soup-Kitchen, as it subsequently became, was feeding fifteen hundred or more.

The rapidity with which a charitable enterprise of any nature is advertised among the people, and the confidence with which the needy throng to the center of assistance recalls the story of the Gospels. Every day from that time until the end of the war, new persons came with their stories of distress, each more heartrending than the last, and within a week there were fifty instead of fifteen to feed; and a few days later one hundred. Mrs. Cortass could no longer feed this crowd from her own door, and the kitchen was moved to a neighbouring French hotel which had been seized, occupied, and then abandoned by Turkish troops. During the remainder of the summer, the food was given out from this place. What this work subsequently became can best be described by a brief account of what it was when I visited it in October, 1917, about fifteen months later.

It was eight o'clock in the morning, a crisp autumn day with a tang in the air that gave one a keen appetite, and made one seek the sunshine. It was the hour for

the morning distribution at the Brummâna Soup-
Kitchen, and the crowd was gathering in a small pine
grove a stone's throw from the distribution shanty.   I
was sitting in this shack watching the preparations for
the distribution.   Men were hurrying from the oven
carrying great basket trays heaped with fragrant
loaves of bread, or staggering along with enormous
cauldrons of steaming gruel.   In a few moments a
young man who was standing just outside the grove
where the crowd was waiting began to read off the list
of names of those regularly enrolled for help; and they
came forward single-file, down a fenced pathway, and
halted before the rail over which the food was served
only long enough to present their tickets and receive
their allotment of gruel and bread.   Each one brought
his own receptacle, and the study of these vessels alone
was ludicrously pathetic.   One had an old battered
enamel pitcher, another a rusty tin pail, another a bis-
cuit box fitted up with a flimsy handle of wire, another an earthenware crock or jar, and still others old
tin cans.   Some of these utensils were large enough to
hold the portions for a family of four or five, others
held only the one huge ladleful that represented a
single portion.

As that tragic line filed past, one of the Syrian
helpers deftly ladled out the gruel, and another handed
out the bread, one loaf for each portion.   Again and
again a fresh kettle of soup or another tray of bread
was brought up to replace the one which had just been
emptied; the distribution lasted nearly an hour.   Out
of the twelve hundred fed that day, nine-tenths were

children, and the rest were women.   For reasons already explained, there were no men or boys over twelve in that line; and fully a fourth of the number who presented their empty buckets to be filled could hardly reach up over the rail, they were so tiny.   Mrs. Dray, who was sitting beside me, watched them all with motherly solicitude, and to each she gave a friendly nod in return for the affectionate *salaams* with which they greeted her.   To some she addressed a question, to others she hinted the advisability of greater cleanliness, or presented a ticket for a new garment.   She knew them all by name and history, and many a fragmentary tragedy she whispered to me as some particularly pathetic individual passed before us. What impressed me most, however, and what most wrung my heart was the frequency with which she would point out some little tot who was entirely alone in the world, the sole survivor of a family of six, eight, or ten individuals.   One had only to examine the face and the figure to estimate how long a person had been fed at the Soup-Kitchen.   Those who had been pensioners for some months were sturdy and wholesome in appearance, and had lost that strained look of anxiety and apprehension.   Those who were newly come were still emaciated, timid, and cowed.   Some were shivering with ague or malaria, others had terrible sore eyes; but each, if only he remained on the Soup-Kitchen list, had the certainty of food and medical care until the end of the war.

At the end of each distribution came the most trying ordeal for those in charge of the relief-work.   There

were never less than fifty stragglers who were not on
the list, but who had assembled with the others in the
hope that any left-overs might fall to their lot.   At
first, whatever remained was distributed as far as it
would go, but in time the number who depended on
sharing this small quantity of food became so great,
and fights over it were so frequent that finally the dis-
tributor had to refuse to give even what was left to any
that were not on the regular list.   It was pitiful to see
the disappointment of the unfortunate ones when they
realized that there was not one drop or one crumb to
spare, and that they could not immediately be enrolled
among the lucky ones.

The food was cooked in enormous cauldrons, and it
was inevitable in the preparation of such a quantity
that a residue should stick to the bottom of the vessel
and char there.   Although this was burned, it contained a certain amount of nutriment, and it was carefully scraped off and given to the two watch-dogs that
guarded the premises.   When the people discovered
this fact they went down on their knees and begged
that it be given to them instead of the dogs, a request
which could not be refused, and they devoured it as
ravenously as the dogs themselves would have done.

Had Dr. Dray obeyed his own great heart, or responded to the full need of that district, he might have
fed fifteen thousand daily; but his funds were limited,
and the most difficult of all the difficult things he had
to do was to turn away those destitute people who besought his aid, and who assured him, all too truly as
he knew, that no one but God and himself could save

them from certain death a few days or weeks hence.
Dr. Dray pled with his treasurer for increased appropriations, and the latter in his turn did his utmost to
obtain contributions from wealthy and influential
friends. But after all, the Brummâna work was only
one of many similar organizations, and the need there,
great as it was, was no greater than that of other districts. A few cases which Dr. Dray cited as typical
reveal the tragedies which resulted from his inability
to increase his work beyond a certain limit.

One day a poor woman visited him in his office in
Beirût. She had five children with her, and all were
manifestly starving. She told the Doctor that her
husband was in the United States, but that she had not
been able to communicate with him, or receive any
financial assistance from him. She stated the simple
fact that they could not live more than a few days
unless some one helped them, and having heard of Dr.
Dray's hospice, she had come to implore him to take
the children in. For herself she asked nothing. She
was ready to die as soon as she knew they were provided for, and she only asked that after the war was
over the Doctor would tell her husband that she had
done her best for her children and his. The hospice
was already full to overflowing, and the Doctor was
turning away daily dozens of similar cases, but he
finally told the mother that he would take two of the
five children. He had no sooner spoken than he saw
his mistake, for the poor mother had then to decide
which of her darlings she should choose. She herself
must appoint the two to live in the knowledge that the

other three would certainly die with her.   Her distress was more than Dr. Dray could bear, and he finally consented to take all five, although he did not know what he could do with them.

In another case, a mother with two children, the only survivors of a family of six or seven little ones, came to him with the same request.   This father also was in America.   The mother would die content, if only the hospice would take her children and Dr. Dray would promise to tell her husband that she had done her best for them.   It was impossible, so it seemed to the Doctor then, to accept another child into the already crowded hospice, but he gave the mother a letter to Azmi Bey recommending her for enrollment in one of the municipal soup-kitchens in Beirût.   It was a cold, rainy day in winter.   The Doctor had walked up to Brummâna to oversee the work, and was hurrying to start back to Beirût before night fell.   About an hour after the woman had left he himself started on the long tramp through the rain.   A short distance out of Brummâna he came upon the mother lying dead by the roadside, her weeping babes shivering beside her. What could he do but turn back to Brummâna taking the children with him?

Such cases as these are what might be called the fortunate ones, for at least certain members of these families were finally enrolled on the Soup-Kitchen list. What, though, of the others for whom there was no room?   Some months later Dr. Dray took me down to a little pine grove on the edge of a precipice not more than thirty yards from the kitchen where the food for distribution was cooked.   In that little clump of trees we found the bones of three people, a woman and two children.   They had died there of starvation with the odour of food in their nostrils, and the wild animals of the hills had eaten their bodies, leaving their bones to whiten on the ground.   That tells the story of thousands.

After the distribution was over, Mrs. Dray took me on a tour of inspection.   The work was located in the extensive grounds of the hotel previously mentioned, and there were two or three hundred employees engaged in preparing the food and maintaining the establishment.   We passed first a shed where about thirty-five women were " stuffing " sheep.   Some were gathering mulberry leaves, or chopping them up fine; others, squatting on the ground hour after hour, crammed the food into the sheeps' mouths.   A sheep fattened in this way soon becomes so heavy that its legs will not bear its weight, and one feels that the process is unnecessarily cruel when one sees the poor beast lying on the ground gasping for breath between swallows, with the inexorable " stuffer " still forcing food down its throat.   At the end of the summer a good fat sheep weighs as much as one hundred or one hundred and fifty pounds before it is butchered, and yields between twenty-five and thirty pounds of dressed meat.   This is salted and preserved in its own fat to be used during the winter when it is difficult to secure fresh meat.

Afterwards we crossed the road and inspected the charcoal kiln where all the fuel used in the kitchens was prepared by the few men who were receiving assistance. The wood for the charcoal was contributed entirely by the beneficiaries of the Soup-Kitchen in partial return for their support. Certain of the men felled the trees, and carried the wood on their backs in some cases for a distance of five, or ten miles, or even more. Others cut it into lengths, and prepared the kilns, over each of which presided a specialist in the art of charcoal manufacture. The output of this branch of the industry was for that season about fifty tons of charcoal, a small portion of which was consumed in the kitchens, while the rest was sold in the market for the maintenance of the relief-work.

Further along was a low shed where fifteen or twenty women were shaping the loaves of bread for the oven. What we know as " Arab bread " is a curious thing. The dough is prepared just as our bread dough, but after kneading it is divided into lumps as large as a woman can hold in one fist. These are set to rise, and then each is patted out into a thin disk about eight inches in diameter and one-eighth of an inch thick. These queer loaves when baked in a very hot oven in close contact with the heat puff up like " popovers," and when cold split naturally into plate-like halves which, when well baked, are thin and crusty. This is the most convenient form of bread in the world. The labourer in Syria lays between the layers the cheese and olives which complete his meal, and thrusts the sandwich inside of his blouse. When he eats, he uses one half as a plate, and pieces of the other for a spoon. There is no compact American picnic-set which can compare with it! An Arab loaf weighs about a quarter of a pound, and contains sufficient nourishment for a meal, if there are other articles on the menu, although a man, or a boy with a healthy appetite, will eat as many as five or six at a time if he can get them. About five thousand loaves were baked every day at the Brummâna Soup-Kitchen, and about half of that number were given out over the rail at the distribution shed. The employees received two loaves for a meal, and a third meal each day for themselves and the members of their immediate families, although the regular distribution provided for only two meals, morning and noon.

By far the most interesting place behind the scenes at the Soup-Kitchen was the stores department. To this Mrs. Cortass, who had assisted Dr. Dray from the very beginning, held the keys. As a matter of fact, although she and her husband had now several hundred employees under them, the entire management of the plant was in their hands—of course under the supervision of Dr. and Mrs. Dray. Wheat, being the principal staple of diet, occupied most of the space in the storehouse, although only a portion of the supply could be kept there at a time, since the normal consumption of the Soup-Kitchen was about a quarter of a ton a day. In upper rooms there were dried vegetables, lentils, beans, and potatoes, with onions, peppers and ochra hanging in festoons on the walls and from the ceiling. In great jars standing on the floor, or in smaller crocks locked away in cupboards, were gallons of a salt tomato ketchup used as seasoning in Syria, by those who can afford it, when fresh vegetables are no longer obtainable; also salted meat made from the fattened sheep. In the Soup-Kitchen these foods were necessities rather than luxuries, for both tomatoes and meat played an important part in the schedule of " balanced rations."

There was a beautifully clean dairy where the milk, cheese and butter were cared for and were prepared for the patients in the hospitals, or the infants in the " babery." The hospice had its own herd of cattle, and Dr. Dray saw to it that the dairy products were handled with proper scientific care and cleanliness.

The food at the Brummâna Soup-Kitchen was prepared with due regard for food-values. The ingredients included the essentials of a wholesome and nutritious diet: fats, proteins, acids, salt, and sugar. Tomatoes and lemons supplied the necessary acid, and were calculated particularly to ward off such diseases as scurvy. Onions were provided as a blood-tonic. Whenever fresh vegetables could be obtained in the market in sufficient quantity and at a reasonable figure they were used freely. The morning that I was there, instead of the usual, and probably monotonous, gruel, eggplants formed the *pièce de résistance*. These the people either roasted in the coals, or ate raw with salt, and they were evidently welcomed as a great delicacy. The noon meal usually consisted of a good, nourishing stew of fresh or dried vegetables cooked with meat and olive oil. Portions were ample, and there was always a loaf of bread with each portion.

We next visited the three hospitals, one for men, one for women, and one for eye-cases, in which student doctors and nurses from the Syrian Protestant College gave the best of medical treatment to any pensioners of the Soup-Kitchen who were in need of special attention.   Dr. Dikran Utidjian was at that time the resident physician, and Dr. Dray is enthusiastic in praise of his management of the medical department. Most of the patients at the time when I was there were suffering from pernicious malaria, scabies, dysentery, or other disorders caused by malnutrition.   There was also an appalling number of cases of ophthalmia, commonly known in Syria as " sore eyes."   There was also an emergency case that morning.   Two of the wood-cutters had got into a fight, and one had received a deep gash across the palm of his hand which necessitated several stitches.   I wondered what the penalty for this misconduct would be, and was told that both contestants would be " laid off " for a week, and would consequently fast and have ample time to repent of their sins.

Last of all we visited the three shelters, for girls, boys, and babies.   In each of the first two there were from forty to sixty children.   Not only did they sleep and eat in the shelters, but they attended classes, graded according to their abilities, exercised in out-of-door play and gymnastic drill, and employed their leisure time in industrial occupations.   The girls spun wool, or made it up into caps, sweaters, stockings or dresses for themselves or their younger brothers and sisters.   The boys learned carpentry and masonry so thoroughly that they were able to build the stone house that later was used as a kitchen.

One of the most touching sights of that visit I saw at noon in the boys' hospice. The lunch of vegetable stew and Arab bread had been spread on long settles, and the children under the leadership of a teacher filed silently into the room, each standing before his own steaming plate. And then, before a spoon was lifted, each bowed his head; and these same children who would have fought each other like savages at the mere sight of food a few months earlier, and who would have devoured it without delay, repeated in unison the Arabic words of the Lord's Prayer.

Before we went to our own luncheon, we stopped to see the distribution of wool to the women workers, and the examination of the finished products. The care with which this department is checked gives a hint of the many possibilities of leakage, but thanks to the Syrian assistants who knew their own people well enough to predict in what directions they might be tempted, and thanks also to Mrs. Dray's shrewdness, this department was conducted with little or no loss, and with enormous benefit to the employees. The wool was assigned to the workers by weight, in quantities sufficient to make a specified article. Each day the worker brought her work to headquarters for inspection; and the garment, as far as she had proceeded, together with the wool still remaining, was weighed and checked with the amount originally assigned. I wondered to see the superintendent run a knitting needle through the ball of yarn, but Mrs. Dray whispered to me that one woman had been caught stealing wool, and substituting a stone to make up the necessary weight. The finished articles, when accepted, were turned in and the worker received a ticket which entitled her to extra food-allowance in lieu of wages. The hospice was very proud of the fact that the most skillful spinner in the whole establishment was a little boy five years old!

This work of Dr. Dray was begun in the summer of 1916 and was continued for thirty months until the American Red Cross arrived in November, 1918, a month after the British occupation, to take over all the relief-work in Syria. The list of beneficiaries included not only residents of Brummâna and adjacent villages, but also the inhabitants of more than fifty other small towns in the vicinity. Some of the pensioners came up daily from Mansuriyeh, about two hours further down the mountain; and the only survivors of that village to-day (about one-fifth of the original population) are those whom Dr. Dray saved either in the Brummâna Soup-Kitchen or by the distribution of funds in the village. Later, as the representatives from outlying villages became more numerous, arrangements were made to send the portion for each to a center in the village, thus saving the inhabitants of more distant places a daily tramp of several weary hours through the mountains. People came to Brummâna from all over the country in the hope of obtaining assistance; and if there were any chance of being enrolled on the Soup-Kitchen list, they camped in the vicinity. The fame of the *Muta'am*, as the Syrians called it, was published throughout the land, and starving people came a great distance to petition for enrollment. Every pauper in Syria seemed to believe that, if only he were in Brummâna, he too would be fed; and pilgrims from distant villages who could not be included in the already over-large list died on the hills about the town.

During the thirty months that Dr. Dray was in charge of this work about four thousand two hundred individuals received assistance for a period of at least two months. Another sixteen hundred might be reckoned in this total, if one counted those who had received help for less than two months. About seventeen hundred was the maximum number that was fed at any one time. More than fifty villages were represented. Nine-tenths of the number were children and the rest women. Perhaps a score of men were paid with food for their labour about the premises. The total sum expended for the Brummâna work was approximately $180,000 for the thirty months, an average of about $105 *per capita*. Considering the price of foodstuffs in Syria during the war, this is a truly remarkable record. Wheat alone, during the later months of the war, was sold in the open market for more than $1,000 a ton, and Dr. Dray's success with the limited sum at his disposal is little short of a miracle.

The first contributions that Dr. Dray received for his relief-work in Brummâna were items of $15, $30, and $75 respectively, that were given him by Mr. Dana from a private fund left with him for special cases that he might wish to help. Later, when the work was organized on a sound basis and bade fair to be a success, he was regularly supplied by Mr. Dana and Mr. Erdman from relief-funds. A private contribution of about $20,000 was raised also among certain wealthy Syrians in Beirût. Although the Brummâna Hospice and Soup-Kitchen may, therefore, be claimed by the American Mission as one of its relief projects, the full credit for its management belongs to Dr. Dray. The idea originated with him, and he contributed largely toward its maintenance from his own pocket, and even more lavishly from his time. He devoted three entire summer-vacations to this work; and during the winter, while he was occupied in Beirût with his collegiate duties, he walked many times each month up to Brummâna to make sure that things were running smoothly. During the winter of 1916, when he himself could not be on the spot all the time, Professor William H. Hall of the Syrian Protestant College, who was temporarily relieved of his teaching responsibilities, took up his residence in Brummâna to supervise the work. The following winter (1917–18) Rev. William A. Freidinger of the American Mission was released by Lebanon Station in order that he might carry on the work which Mr. Hall had so ably conducted the previous year. During the whole of the thirty months of its existence, however, the Brummâna work was Dr. Dray's special responsibility, and he was the only director whom the government officials would recognize. Hence it fell to him to make all the necessary arrangements in connection with procuring supplies, or dealing otherwise with the Turkish officials.

In addition to Mr. Hall and Mr. Freidinger, Dr. Dray was fortunate in his associates. His Syrian assistants were indefatigable in their efforts for the success of the enterprise, and all who profited by the relief owe a special debt of gratitude to Mr. and Mrs. Cortass, who bore a large share of the responsibility of the management. Dr. Utidjian and his assistants in the hospitals have already been mentioned, and there were many other loyal helpers who contributed generously to the success of the work.

After the occupation Dr. Dray transferred his relief unit over to the American Red Cross, which, in turn, handed it over to the Syria and Palestine Relief Fund. The orphanage has been continued, but it is a considerable disappointment to Dr. Dray, and to those interested in his work, that the flourishing industrial department has been abandoned. This great enterprise has to-day dwindled to insignificant proportions; and the Brummâna work, once famous all over Syria, is now of no special interest or importance.

It was a peculiar fact that the very government officials who were most determinedly bent on exterminating the Syrian people vied with each other in their patronage of the Brummâna Relief-Work. Jemal Pasha regarded this work as his own special protégé, and the Governor of Beirût, not to be outdone by his great rival, was also pleased to favour it. Tahsin Bey, Governor of Damascus, from whose district most of the wheat used in Brummâna was purchased, and Ali Munif, and his successor, Ismail Hakki Bey, the Governors of Lebanon, also visited and commended the work. On one occasion three Governors of Turkish provinces made a special trip to visit the work and consented to be photographed with certain members of the relief-staff. This visit of these three Governors marks a great event in the history of the Brummâna Soup-Kitchen.

There were many other soup-kitchens and hospices under American management in Syria, in various districts in Lebanon, and in Tripoli and Sidon. Most of these were patterned after Dr. Dray's model, and therefore need not be described in detail. In the Sidon district a soup-kitchen was organized and managed by Mr. and Mrs. Stuart D. Jessup. This provided for one hundred and fifty children throughout the winter of 1916–17. Four sub-kitchens in outlying districts were later established and superintended by other members of the American Mission in Sidon, thus increasing the number of beneficiaries to about four hundred.

. In Sûk-el-Gharb, Lebanon, Mr. George Scherer conducted another soup-kitchen along similar lines, and during the last two years of the war it is estimated that he provided for about three thousand people, the majority of whom were children.

Mr. Bayard Dodge of the Syrian Protestant College, previously mentioned as a member of the Red Cross Executive Committee, and now a member of the Permanent Committee for American Relief in Syria, supported about twelve thousand individuals from funds that he personally contributed. His central kitchen was in 'Abeih, Lebanon, which supplied scores of villages in the district; and he had extensive charitable interests in other localities. There is a cluster of picturesque villages perched on the steep mountainside back of Shemlân which to-day owe their very existence to Mr. "Dudj," and any one who knew the history of American relief in Syria might point out to the traveller dozens of other towns which he has saved.

It need not be explained that such extensive relief activities required not only a tremendous financial backing, but also enormous purchases of supplies, especially wheat. How the American Mission expended hundreds of thousands of dollars in relief, believing that it would one day be reimbursed by the relief societies in America, and how that faith was soon justified by the announcement of a regular monthly appropriation from the Armenian and Syrian Relief Committee has already been described. The tale of the way in which the necessary supplies were secured would constitute a chapter in itself, and a thrilling one at that, but there is no space here to describe it in detail. In the summer of 1917 these purchases for relief-work became so large that the Government grew alarmed and determined to put a stop to such extensive activities. The *Vâli* of Beirût arrested Mr. Dana, who was directing the relief-work in Syria, and ordered his deportation. Later in Constantinople Mr. Dana was accused of acting as the agent of the enemy in the purchase of supplies in preparation for an enemy advance. This was the first intimation that he received as to the form of the trumped-up charge against him. Fortunately there were able successors to carry on the relief program which he had instituted, and the work proceeded without further interruption until the British occupation of Syria less than a year later.

XIV

THE DEPORTATION AND IMPRISONMENT OF THE DIRECTOR OF AMERICAN RELIEF IN SYRIA

THERE is only one thing of which you can always be sure in Turkey—that the unexpected will certainly happen. The summer of 1917 was, on the surface, uneventful, yet we felt all the time that something would surely occur; and when the actual crash came, it seemed more or less the expected thing. Practically all the Americans left Beirût for the mountains that summer. There was little coming and going between the city and the various mountain homes because conveyances were few and prohibitive in price. We had scarcely any excitements, save watching an occasional aeroplane bomb the city, or seeing British cruisers shell the German benzine depot near the port. We heard constant rumours of a possible landing on the coast. There seemed, in that event, little likelihood of an advance being made into the mountains, which were somewhat fortified, and, in 1917, contained a number of troops. However welcome an invasion would have been, we might have found ourselves cut off from friends and funds in Beirût, in which case we should have had the choice of trying to run the gauntlet into the Entente lines, or of facing indefinite isolation on the Turkish side. This thought provided food for speculation for those who cared to indulge in it. However, the summer passed quietly.

The autumn was an unusually mild one, and we decided to stay in 'Aleih where we had been spending the summer until after Thanksgiving Day, November 29th. It is futile, however, in Turkey, to plan for more than a day ahead. On November 19th, immediately upon his return to Beirût after a week-end visit in 'Aleih, Mr. Dana was arrested by six policemen. Our house was searched, and all papers were confiscated. The Press safes and files were likewise examined. Mr. Dana was then imprisoned in his own house. Friends in Beirût warned us not to try to communicate with him; but fortunately his Syrian secretary, under the pretext of bringing him food, acted as messenger for the exchange of tiny notes and verbal communications during the week's imprisonment. Saturday night, after six days of suspense, we received the joyful news that Mr. Dana's papers had been examined by the police and pronounced innocuous. We assumed that he would be released without further delay. On Sunday morning, however, Professor Crawford brought us word that, although Mr. Dana had been liberated from immediate confinement, he had been sentenced to exile from Syria. It was left to his choice whether his family should accompany him; and although he had not decided whether it would be advisable to take us, he asked us to return to Beirût with the least possible delay. After three hours of feverish packing and dismantling the house we left for the city.

When Mr. Dana was arrested, we had feared the worst; and a mere deportation under liberal restrictions was a distinct relief. Azmi Bey had positively refused to give any reasons for his action. His only comment was: " You have many enemies." The chief among them was doubtless then sitting in Azmi's own chair. The Prefect of Police, Mukhtar Bey, when asked by the Governor to sign Mr. Dana's deportation order, expressed great surprise, because he said the police had found no charge against Mr. Dana, and he knew no cause for his deportation. What the full truth of the affair was we did not learn until seven months later in Constantinople.

Mr. Dana asked for a week in which to arrange his business affairs, but Azmi replied, " You may have three days." The American remembered that on the fourth day Jemal Pasha was expected in town, and he suspected that Azmi wished to leave him no opportunity of appealing to the Pasha for a reversal of the unreasonable sentence. Then followed hectic days of preparation. Mr. Dana was forced to devote all his time to business affairs, and scarcely stopped to eat, or to see the scores of callers who came to say good-bye or to help us in our preparations.

At four o'clock on Thanksgiving morning, after only an hour's sleep, and while it was still dark, we left our home to return we knew not when. Our party consisted of Mr. and Mrs. Dana, three-year-old Dorothy, myself, and the servant, who had elected to share our fortunes. We had to condense our winter-clothing, bedding, and food into baggage which we could ourselves carry if need be. Our immediate destination was Konia in the heart of Anatolia, with the possibility of Constantinople or Smyrna as a permanent residence. Our journey from Beirût to Constantinople was prolonged to nearly two months. It is a tale by itself with many amusing and many trying incidents.

The train-service over Lebanon was closed to civilians, so we left Beirût in a German freight-lorry, perched on top of our baggage. After a series of delays we reached Reyâk, the junction with the Aleppo railroad. The journey which should have taken five hours at the most had occupied thirteen, with a climate that varied from an Indian-summer day to a cold winter night. At Reyâk there was no hotel, only shelter from the bitter wind in a tiny, unfurnished shack, intended, so we were told, as a rest-house for Turkish officers' wives! The next morning we were greatly relieved to find that a freight-train would leave for Aleppo before noon, so we crawled into an empty box-car and set up light housekeeping. A freight-car, if you can have one reserved for your party, is far preferable in Turkey to the crowded, unsanitary passenger-coaches, and we realized for the first time the luxuries of real " hobo " life in a " side-door Pullman."

Dorothy's illness from exposure and our need of purchasing supplies for the rest of the journey delayed us for a week in Aleppo, so that it was ten days after we had left Beirût before we were again *en route*.

We had the greatest difficulty in finding places on the north-bound train, but were happy and comfortable for twelve hours in our hard-won quarters. At half-past nine at night the police removed us from the train at Marmoureh, a little village high in the Amanus Mountains. We were taken through ankle-deep mud and pouring rain to the police station, where our permits were examined and our hand-baggage thoroughly searched. Our heavy baggage escaped the overhauling as we had checked it through to Kelibek. The train had gone on without us, and as there was no other due until the next morning we were kept all night in the police station where we tried without success to sleep on the hard chairs. The only one who slept at all occupied the top of the commissaire's office-table. The next morning we huddled into a car on a freight-train bound for Adana, where we rested two days with the missionaries then resident in the American School. There were only three in the city at that time, Dr. Cyril H. Haas, Miss Towner, and Miss Davies. We left Adana two mornings later at the unholy hour of two o'clock; and in the darkness and scramble, our food-bag and kerosene stove were stolen. We had almost despaired of finding places on the train when some German soldiers invited us to share their accommodations in a Red Cross car. These soldiers, one of whom was an American citizen caught in Germany at the beginning of the war and forced into the army, proved very friendly, and helped us at Kelibek to secure places in the Taurus narrow-gauge train. We were lucky in the weather that we encountered on the

Taurus trip. It was a lovely, winter day, and the beautiful ride through the mountains made up for many hardships.

When we reached Karapounar, the northern terminus of the great Taurus tunnel, we found that traffic toward Konia had been greatly congested by heavy blizzards along the line. The town was crowded with a four days' accumulation of travellers, and there was no hotel. We were fortunate enough to find places for the night in the *Soldatenheim,* where we were tolerated because we had a small child with us, but were treated with scant courtesy. The ground was covered with snow, and that night was bitterly cold.

The next day there was a north-bound train, but it could not begin to accommodate the hundreds who gathered with their baggage at the station. We fought our way through an ugly crowd into a third-class car, the only one into which we could penetrate. However, we were too glad to escape from Karapounar to grumble at our accommodations. Half an hour later, at Bozanti, we were again taken to the police station for examination of our permits and baggage. At every turn one had to show permits, and ours were always scrutinized with extra care. A two-hour stop was made there, but that time was barely sufficient for the police formalities, and we only just got back into our places before the train started.

About twelve hours later we ran into a blizzard, and at daybreak found that our train was stalled on a bleak, wind-swept plateau, near Karaman, with snow two feet deep. We were delayed forty-five hours, just three hours south of Konia. All watering stations along the line were frozen solid. The weather ranged between thirty-two and twenty degrees below zero. The train was unheated. We had lost our stove and most of our provisions, and we lived on sweet chocolate and cookies for several meals. The last evening we were grateful for the gift of some frozen boiled potatoes which a Greek family traded with us for drinking water, with which we were well supplied. The morning of the first day after we were storm-bound, we saw the stiffened corpses of nine people carried out of the train and thrown into an open coal-car. There was one German soldier, several Turkish soldiers, and some Moslem women and children. The second morning the pile in the coal-car was increased by eleven (two from our own car), and the third morning twelve were added, making a total of thirty-two. As we watched those ghastly processions during those three days, it was a question in our minds how soon one of us would suffer the same fate.

The thirty-hour trip from Adana to Konia took us in all six days, during which time we never had our coats off, or lay down for a single night. We had only two warm meals. We dared not face the risk of enduring more cold on the bleak plateau beyond Konia, so we decided to break our journey at that point. It was well that we did this, for we were all ill with heavy colds, and Dorothy's developed into pneumonia. Had it not been for the kindness of Miss Cushman, an American missionary who took us into her home, I do not believe that the little girl would have won in the fight that she made for her life. We spent more than a month at Konia, a picturesque and typically Turkish town, and we had there our only glimpse into the real life of the interior of Anatolia. We had also the pleasure of meeting Mr. Dana's assistant in the Press, Mr. Henry Glockler, who was a British interned civilian in Bey Chehir, and who had obtained permission to visit us for a few days.

Five weeks after our arrival at Konia we were again on our way. The rest of the trip occupied only three days, and was luxurious compared with our previous experiences in travel, for we had a cushioned compartment all to ourselves. Our greatest asset was a neat, new travelling permit, secured from the *Vāli* of Konia who, being a special enemy of Azmi Bey, was pleased to thwart him by disguising the fact that we were exiles. This ruse helped us to evade the Constantinople police, who, for six months, were unable to locate the dangerous characters from Beirût. We heard from friends of their repeated efforts to trace us both in Konia and in the Capital.

We reached the Haidar Pasha terminus of the Anatolian Railway late on a Saturday night, but could not leave the train until early the next morning, January 20th, when we crossed the Bosphorus and entered the Capital. We had been just fifty-two days from the time we left Beirût, although in point of actual miles the journey is not much further than from New York to Omaha! No wonder, after the dreary weeks in the interior, that, when we first saw the Marmora, like

Xenophon's men, we wanted to shout, " The sea, the sea! "

I fear that our first impressions of Constantinople were merely relevant to creature comforts. On our drive from the ferry to the hotel we were thrilled with the sensation of being again in a real metropolis with tall buildings and big shops. There seemed an amazing amount of meat, vegetables, fruits, and—rarer still to our recent experience—candies and cakes   Months later, remembering those first hours in the city, we felt sympathy for some German soldiers who were coming along the *Grande Rue de Pera.* They had evidently just arrived on the *Balkanzug* from Germany. One of them hailed excitedly a friend on the other side of the street: "Ach, Fritz, Fritz! Komm' 'mal her. Ach, die Kuchen, die Kuchen! " (Fritz, Fritz, come here. Oh the cakes, the cakes!) Constantinople was specially favoured in these respects because public sentiment was so strong against the war that the Germans and the Turks found it necessary to keep the city well provisioned in order to avoid possible revolutionary protests from the pacifists.

The ruthless extravagance of the Constantinople population, especially the newly-rich, was something appalling. Those who had money squandered it in a most shameless fashion, and the merchants were not slow to take advantage of this spendthrift spirit. Silk gloves and stockings imported from Vienna sold at $10 to $15 a pair. Cakes at $8 a pound, chocolates at $25 a pound, and shoes of native manufacture at $75 a pair. An after-theatre supper for four persons, with sandwiches, wine and champagne, cost $500, and the waiter's tip in proportion!

When we presented ourselves at Tokatlian's Hotel in Pera, the Management hesitated before assigning us rooms, such a bedraggled, unshorn appearance did we all present. For days after our arrival we revelled in the rejuvenation produced by hot water, steam-heated rooms, delicious meals, and the mere enjoyment of life in a cosmopolitan center. We felt ourselves in touch with the world again through daily papers, even if they represented only the German viewpoint. It was good to be in a metropolis once more. Yet it never really seemed the Constantinople that we had pictured either in memory or in imagination. To Marion Crawford, to Pierre Loti, to the scores of people who have known and written about the city, it was something different. In their day, the old bazaars with their blue and gold ceilings were gay with silks, rugs, embroideries, and pottery. The people themselves were clad in fanciful colours; veiled women in many-hued silk wraps, and men with red fezzes, green or white turbans, and bright silk belts. Greeks, Georgians, Montenegrins, Croats in their striking national garb, jostled one another on the Galata Bridge, the main artery of the city. The harbour and the Golden Horn were crowded with gay-coloured craft. The city, piled on the hills on either side, was touched with every tint that the soul of an artist could desire. Altogether Constantinople of the past left the impression of something distinctly unique and colourful.

Not so in the years of the war. The bazaars of

Stamboul had been damaged by fire, and but few brightly decorated parts remained, while all were woefully bereft of picturesque wares. They were still interesting, but almost too unsanitary from the presence of second-hand goods exposed for sale to let one risk many visits. There were very few mysterious, veiled women in loose outer garments of silk. In fact, a surprising number of Moslem women had discarded the veil entirely. The prevailing colour in the crowds was a dirty brown, black or gray. Brown was the general effect of the shoddy Turkish uniforms. Black was the sombre costumes of the women, with the short cape, or *charshaf,* over the head and shoulders; or the fezzes of the men, dyed dark for mourning. Gray was the German and Austrian uniforms. The garb of all harmonized and blended with the prevailing fog and general wretchedness of the city. Every fourth person who passed our hotel was a soldier. The Germans were very much in evidence, and the Turks made no secret of their jealousy and hatred of them. The Austrians were less overbearing in manner, and were on better terms with their Oriental allies. A short visit which Emperor Charles and Empress Rita made to Constantinople in the early summer further cemented this cordial feeling. The populace gave them an enthusiastic welcome and was charmed by their gracious simplicity of bearing.

Save for the foreign element, the average crowd in Constantinople was stunted in size and most depressingly depraved in appearance. The whole city was ill-kempt, and poorly administered. Even its monuments of the past, the fine mosques, adapted from early Christian churches, which are its only glory so far as public buildings are concerned, were desecrated by the filthy hordes of Turkish soldiers who were quartered in them.

This is a pessimistic picture of the Capital, but it was true only so far as the hand of the Turk rested upon it in the last days of the struggle of a dying Empire. The physical beauty of its location can never be wholly marred by the hand of man, and is its redeeming feature now that the glory of the past has faded. Nature has done her utmost to make up for the deficiencies of the Turks; especially in the matter of flowers she has been lavish, and she has seemed to single out the most shabby and ramshackle buildings to support masses of wistaria which, in early summer, glorify even the dingiest quarter of the city.

In early spring we moved from the city to Constantinople College, where Mr. Dana had been asked to act as Treasurer. This institution, formerly known as the American College for Girls, occupies a wonderful site above the village of Arnaoutkeuy, on the upper Bosphorus, about an hour by tram from the heart of Constantinople. Its exceptionally beautiful and well-equipped buildings are situated on a charming campus. Mr. Dana spent part of his time in the College, and the remainder in the city attending to whatever affairs of the Mission and Press he could manage from a distance. Through our association with the Girls' College, and through Mr. Dana's interests in the city we became acquainted with a great many interesting people. In Robert College, also, and the American Mission we soon found congenial friends, many of whom, like ourselves, were, through the fortunes of war, only temporary residents in the city. These friendships were a great help in time of need, and now form the pleasantest memories of our stay in Constantinople.

On July first, we were visiting at Robert College when word came that Dr. William S. Nelson of Tripoli, Syria, had arrived in Stamboul. About the time of our departure from Beirût we had heard that Dr. Nelson also was experiencing some difficulties with the Turks. Later we learned that he had been deported from Syria, and ordered to the interior of Anatolia. At Adana he had discovered an old friend among the police, and had succeeded in spending the winter with the American missionaries there, before the Constantinople police finally located him and ordered him to appear before the Court Martial in the Capital.

Mr. Fowle, American Attaché to the Swedish Legation, in charge of American interests, and Mr. Dana immediately called at the address Dr. Nelson had sent them, not knowing that he was then under police guard. They had half an hour with him, during which they learned why he had been deported. An hour later he was taken to the Military Prison at the War Department. A *kavass* was sent from the Swedish Legation to inquire about his welfare, but was roughly repulsed, and for three and a half months he was kept in a dingy cell, and was not allowed to communicate with any one.

Azmi Bey regarded Dr. Nelson as another of his special enemies because of his prominence in relief-work in the Tripoli, Ḥomṣ and Ḥamâ region. The same week that Mr. Dana was arrested, Dr. Nelson's private residence in Ḥomṣ had been seized by the Turks, and his personal effects had been confiscated. He had sent a special messenger with a note to Mr. Dana requesting him to bring this violation of previous agreements in regard to American property to the attention of the Dutch Consul General in Beirût. The messenger was intercepted, and Azmi seized upon this incident as a pretext for arresting Dr. Nelson, and accusing him of suspicious conduct. He was imprisoned for a month in Tripoli, and later deported to the interior during the worst winter weather. He suffered much ill-treatment, being kept in foul prisons with common criminals in several places *en route*. Immediately upon Dr. Nelson's arrival and imprisonment, Mr. Dana had reason to expect a similar fate, and though he generously spared us his suspicions, he made all his preparations with this in mind.

Two weeks later, on July 14th, six military and civil police arrived at the College. Our rooms were thoroughly searched, and Mr. Dana was carried off, whither we knew not, or why. We later learned that he spent two nights in one of the awful secret prisons of Stamboul, without food or water. There were more than thirty criminals in the one small cell, and they were so packed together that none had space either to lie or sit. Some of the prisoners had apparently been there many days, and one of a group of eight who were chained to the wall with their hands above their heads died the first night, and was still hanging there in a bloated condition when, two days later, Mr. Dana was removed to the Military Prison in the War Department. There he was put for a few hours into an underground dungeon, but was subsequently removed to a cell in the main prison. This cell already contained an Egyptian spy, a nephew of the Sultan, who had killed a comrade in a drunken brawl, and an insane Turk. The latter soon became obsessed with the idea that the newcomer had been sent to assassinate him, and during the next month made three attempts to cut his throat when he supposed him to be sleeping. For one week Mr. Dana was practically without food, and was allowed only a small quantity of water once a day. He suffered from dysentery, but was refused medical aid of any nature. He had no bed, and the vermin and rats were a constant annoyance. When we succeeded in finding out where he was, we made vain attempts to see him. We were put off with promises, and with lies about an excellent restaurant which once existed near the prison, and from which prisoners who were able to pay were said to obtain meals. We did not know that this restaurant was a myth, and that all his money had been taken away from him when he entered the prison. After a week an accommodating Albanian guard who had worked in a hotel in New York smuggled out to us a note from the prisoner asking for food, which we at once sent.

Gradually we got an entering wedge into the prison.

Precedent is everything in Turkey; and although we were not permitted to see Mr. Dana the first three times when we called, when the officials got accustomed to the sight of us, we were allowed to come and go quite as a matter of course. The same was true of the able young *kavass* from the Swedish Legation who accompanied us as courier and interpreter, and who was permitted to carry to the prisoner the food and water which we sent him three times a week. The Egyptian cellmate also proved a good friend, and sometimes loaned Mr. Dana his brazier for cooking or boiling water. While food, water, books, and clean laundry reached him, they only slightly mitigated the discomfort of his surroundings. Day and night he was never out of hearing of the clank of chains in the dungeons below, or the groans of other unfortunates who were being beaten, often until they died. The prison was unspeakably filthy, and was infested with vermin.

One night there stood as guard at the cell door a man who spoke Arabic. This fact was so unusual in a place where only Turkish was known that Mr. Dana made bold to address him. It seemed little short of a miracle that this soldier had been recruited recently from a village near Beirût, and more wonderful still that his last appeal in behalf of his family which he was leaving destitute had been to the American Press. He recognized the Press Manager in the prisoner, and urged him to flee. He was surprised that no greater advantage was taken of his assistance than a quiet exit to the courtyard, where, in a stone watering trough, Mr. Dana had his first bath in many weeks. Save on that occasion, and on one other when he was taken a few paces across the compound to the War Department, he was never out of his tiny cell for over seven weeks.

Every moonlight night and on special holidays Constantinople was subjected to British aeroplane raids. One of the main objectives was the War Department Building adjacent to the prison. One bomb destroyed two large anti-aircraft guns in the yard just below Mr. Dana's window, killed several guards, and wounded prisoners in the rooms on either side of his, but no shrapnel entered his cell.

During all the time while Mr. Dana and Dr. Nelson were undergoing these nerve-racking experiences we were seeking through every channel to find out the charge against them, and to learn how the case would proceed. The War Department was a close secret-society, and Enver Pasha, the well-known head of the coterie, was particularly inaccessible and was much feared. His second, Seifi Bey, was not much more approachable. No Turk could be induced to meddle even indirectly with War Department affairs lest he incur its ill-will. There were no American men in Constantinople who were in a position to help us otherwise than through advice and sympathy, so Mrs. Dana and I were obliged to manage as best we could by ourselves. Fortunately we had a large circle of acquaintances, and we were fairly familiar with the city. With almost every one we used French as a medium, and we found the direct method of personal visits or letters usually more effective than dependence upon others. A typical instance of this was our success in getting the insane man removed from Mr. Dana's cell. After trying three weeks through five different channels, we finally accomplished it by a call, and a letter in most flowery English addressed by Mrs. Dana to the Commandant de la Place who had authority over the Warden of the Prison.

We were often impressed by the lack of coördination in the various departments of the Turkish police. This was because they had only a crude imitation of the German system. Though Mr. Dana was so carefully guarded, letters were still delivered for him at the usual address. After the first fifteen days of his imprisonment we were allowed to see him, but our first visit was very brief and in the presence of an interpreter. As the Turks never give women credit for any intelligence, we were regarded as quite harmless; the following week the interpreter was present for only part of our stay, and never at any time afterwards. We knew that none of the persons usually in the Commandant's office understood English. I took advantage of this fact to report the contents of letters and telegrams to my chief, and he gave me instructions as to replies, and other business affairs. Thus all the time that he was closely immured he was able to direct certain matters affecting the relief-work which had been the chief cause of all his difficulties.

The Swedish Legation to which American interests were entrusted was frankly pronounced by some Germans in that Embassy as more pro-German and anti-American than the Germans themselves. Although

the matter of the detention of two Americans at the
Military Prison should properly have been referred immediately to the Military Attaché of the Swedish
Legation as the proper person to communicate with
the Minister of War, it was not even brought to his
attention until the eve of his departure for Switzerland. The Swedish Minister was absent on leave, and
the Counsellor who was acting in his absence did not
feel inclined to take active interest in so complicated a
case. So far as we knew, he mentioned the imprisonment of Dr. Nelson and Mr. Dana in only one official
visit to the Minister of Foreign Affairs. The only
response was that such a matter should be referred
to the Minister of War. Furthermore, the Counsellor
flatly refused to report the matter to the State Department at Washington, and would not even forward
the telegram which we ourselves drew up requesting
the State Department to inform the Presbyterian
Board of Foreign Missions of the fate of two of its
missionaries. About a week before Mr. Dana was set
at liberty, they finally yielded to our importunity to the
extent of reporting the matter by letter, which probably reached the State Department about two months
later—some time after the Turkish Armistice was
signed.

Mr. Dana's release on September 3rd came as suddenly as his arrest. Up to the very moment when it
occurred, not ten minutes after we had left the prison
very downhearted after one of our weekly visits, we
had not the slightest intimation of any such possibility.
We knew he had been summoned before the Court

Martial on several occasions. We also understood that the findings of the court regarding his case had been handed to Seifi Bey, Enver's second, and that any resultant action rested now with the sweet will of that man, who might take two days or two years before he made up his mind, and in the end might either liberate or execute the prisoner according to his mood on the day when he made the decision.

We now know that we owe Mr. Dana's release to our friend, Captain Arthur von Haas, Naval Attaché of the German Embassy, who was personally acquainted with Seifi Bey, and who told him in strong terms that, if Turkey considered herself a civilized nation, she should either try and punish that American or dismiss him. Dr. Nelson was not released until October 18th, six weeks later, when the Turks began to realize that they were playing a losing game, and wanted to propitiate American sentiment.

During the five months of Mr. Dana's stay in Constantinople before he was located by the police, he came into contact through financial matters with Djavid Bey, Minister of Finance, with Ali Munif Bey, former Governor of Lebanon, then Minister of Public Works, and with others in official circles. Ali Munif Bey was one of the persons who was exceedingly courteous and friendly to us during our difficulties, and did what he could to help. Early in 1918 some questions arose in official circles in Constantinople as to Azmi Bey's conduct in office, and Mr. Dana was able to furnish facts regarding certain cases of bribery and blackmail in which Azmi was the principal. In the early summer, Azmi Bey was dismissed from office, and after he had loitered about a month in Beirût on the pretence of closing up his affairs there, he obeyed the summons from Constantinople. He knew that Mr. Dana was the one person in Constantinople cognizant of certain of his misdeeds, and for revenge he sent false papers to the Capital which caused the revival of the deportation question, Dr. Nelson's further deportation to Constantinople, and the imprisonment of both Americans. He thereby caused a great deal of distress until the endless ramifications of Turkish injustice could be disentangled.

During all this time local history in Constantinople was in the making. The old Sultan, Mahmoud V, had died on July 4th, and had been succeeded by Mahmoud Reshad, a man of wholly different calibre. Those who saw him said that he had a calm, dignified bearing, and a frank, piercing glance. He soon showed a tendency to disregard time-honoured customs, especially as to the seclusion of the Sultan. His first act of self-assertion was to attend the funeral of his brother, the late Sultan, a simple act of family affection which outraged all imperial traditions. He allowed petitioners to approach him on the street, and he even went so far as to plan an office for himself in the War Department where he could see people on business during business hours. He went in person to several of the awful fires, kindled by incendiaries as a protest against the war, which raged in Constantinople that summer, and destroyed a quarter of the Stamboul area. The Triumvirate, who were accustomed to a mere figurehead as ruler, soon realized that they had a different problem on their hands. The new Sultan had his own ideas about governing, and he postponed for weeks the ceremony of the Sword Investiture, which is equivalent to a coronation, until he had been able to enforce certain much-needed reforms. The Committee of Union and Progress endeavoured to keep him practically a prisoner in his palace, but the reaction against that party had already set in, and the scheme to control the new Sultan resulted in the overthrow of the Cabinet and the establishment of another, presumably chosen from the peace party. This marked the greatest day in Turkey's history in over ten years. For a decade the Triumvirate had held complete sway, but now the mighty had fallen.

During the first half of 1918 the Germans evidently felt that they still had control of the situation in the Ottoman Empire, even though they realized that Turkey—that is to say the Young Turks—proved a refractory ally. They had been successful in duping the Turks to the point of making them believe that the management of affairs was in Ottoman hands, and that the Teutonic rôle was merely to suggest up-to-date methods. The newspapers which manifestly were either subsidized by Germany, or were in deadly fear of German censorship, had a good deal to say about Turkey's wonderful progress in the past three years, the tremendous development of her natural resources, and her glorious share in the ultimate triumph of her Prussian allies. The Germans who inspired the Ottoman Press did their utmost to inflame Turkish enmity, which was all too slow to kindle, against the Americans. The *Osmanische Lloyd* published several impassioned attacks against the American missionaries and educational institutions in Turkey, which they designated as the agents of American political propaganda. There was always war news too—on the first page in those days—and lots of pictures, some of them fakes, posted in the official news bureaus. Constantinople was probably the one place in the world where news of events everywhere was freely disseminated. We knew from hour to hour what was happening, not only in Germany and Bulgaria, but also in England, Egypt, France and America. The news from the fronts was, so far as we could judge, practically correct, but so carefully worded that, unless one studied the map from day to day, one could not be sure just which way the real success pointed. Germany and Turkey, it was interesting to note, were never defeated anywhere, but always " withdrew to a stronger position for strategic reasons." The morale of the Entente forces was always at its last ebb, and the American army was despicable, and could not contain any decent men, since it had enlisted, as facts attested, such absolute riff-raff as 13,000 negroes, some of whom were even officers! Scarcely a day passed without some reference to the fact that in England and America there were strong parties opposed to the war, and the I. W. W. and Sinn Fein outbursts were quoted liberally as instances of popular feeling. Many of the items were most laughable. Yet we watched also with anxious eyes the apparent failure of the Entente spring drive in France, and the slow progress in Palestine.

Then in September it seemed as though everything began to happen at once. We watched the disintegration of Bulgaria and the moral collapse in Germany. Word came of the sweeping advance of British forces in Syria and of the British occupation of Beirût on October 8th. Soon Germans and Austrians whom we had known in Syria began to arrive in Constantinople with varying tales of their flight. The Bulgarian Armistice was signed on September 30th. The Turkish Cabinet again fell, and a new cabinet made definite overtures for an armistice. Following the success of their negotiations, but before the Entente forces entered Constantinople, Enver, Talaat, Jemal, Azmi, Bedri, and all their most guilty associates fled the city. Those were exciting days with the front pages of the papers given to discussion of the terms of the impending treaty, and the war news relegated to chance items on the last page. The populace went mad when the Armistice was signed, and the whole city blossomed with flags of every nationality. We had never seen such a demonstration on any other occasion during our stay. All, save the Germans, Austrians, and the few Turks who possessed some national pride, gave themselves up to rejoicing. It was a gladsome holiday, not a day of defeat.

Those last two months in Constantinople, after the signing of the Armistice, were in some respects by far the most agreeable of our stay in that city. There was a sense of relief from the terrible uncertainty, and we knew that with the changed conditions we were freed from further persecution at the hand of the Turks. Up to the very last, the Government created the misleading impression that the terms of the Armistice with Turkey were much more favourable than those with Bulgaria. They stated in positive terms that there was to be no occupation of the city, but that the Ottoman Government had consented to open the Straits for the passage of the Entente fleet to the Black Sea. A small commission of British officers might take up their quarters in the Capital, as that was a convenient base for operations against Russia. Consequently, when, after the Dardanelles had been swept of mines, seventy-six warships steamed across the Marmora and anchored in the Bosphorus with every apparent intention of remaining there, it made a profound impression. The Turkish enthusiasts hardly knew what to say. A few hours later several thousand British troops landed and marched through the streets, acclaimed and showered with flowers by the non-Turkish elements—another distinct surprise to a large part of the population. Whatever Turkish illusions had been, it was evident to the impartial observer that the Turkish Armistice amounted to a treaty of complete surrender. The forts on the Dardanelles and the Bosphorus were occupied by Entente forces; the Turks were obliged to restore all foreign institutions which they had seized; the Germans and Austrians were interned as prisoners of war, and once more Constantinople, even if still under a Moslem Sultan, was practically in control of a Christian government.

Materially the city at once showed the effects of the occupation by a change for the worse. The Turks then realized for the first time that they had been dependent on their allies for many of the necessities of life. White flour, brought from Germany and Austria at the expense of the populations of these countries to keep up a good appearance in the Turkish Capital, was immediately at a premium. Railroad connection with Europe had already been severed by the Bulgarian Armistice, and now there was no German wireless to bring news to Constantinople. Germans who had been superintending the mines on the Black Sea coast flooded them before their departure, and there was no longer enough coal to provide the city with adequate electricity for lighting, running the printing presses and tramcars, or for the Bosphorus steamers. Worst of all, the water-pumping station was completely out of fuel. The Entente had neither the means nor the inclination to help Turkey while she was learning the lesson of her own inadequacy. The Entente fleet could not even coal its own ships satisfactorily at Constantinople, and there were more important projects afoot than the rehabilitation of an enemy capital.

Lawlessness ran rife in the city. The civilians clashed with the military. Greeks, Turks, and Armenians seized this opportunity to settle long-standing grievances, and every day literally dozens of mutilated bodies were found in the side-streets. No one dared step outside of his house after dark, unless he were accompanied by four or five others, and all were heavily armed. The employees of concerns which kept late hours, like the newspapers, were particularly subject to attack, although there seemed no other motive than race-hatred for these deeds of violence.

Consequently, before we left at the end of December, we had experienced the inconveniences of life in a city which had only erratic lighting, no tramcars, few boats, water for an hour or so daily in the lower levels, irregular newspapers; and where the prices of such staples as meat, flour and vegetables were continually soaring. Also the third epidemic of Spanish influenza in six months was raging, and the usual winter typhus and typhoid were on the increase. Mrs. Dana and Dorothy were both victims of the " flu " in a light form, which prevented our leaving with Mr. Dana.

While the Armistice was still under discussion it occurred to the Turks that it might be advisable to release the belligerent subjects whom they held as interns in the interior. Some of these returned to their former residences in the country; others congregated in Constantinople and Smyrna, where they hoped to obtain passage for England and France. Our friend, Henry Glockler, who had been interned at Bey Chehir, joined us in Constantinople; and on December 1st he, Mr. Dana, and Dr. Nelson left by train for Salonika, *via* Bulgaria. What should have been a thirty-hour railroad journey took these men six days of considerable hardship, and constitutes a little adventure by itself. "All's well that ends well," however, and they reached Egypt in time for Christmas. Dr. Nelson left for Syria the latter part of December. The rest of us, Mrs. Dana, Dorothy and I, delayed at Constantinople until we could travel by sea. Through the never-failing courtesy of the British officials, we succeeded in getting passage on the *Kashgar*, a British transport, and had a most luxurious trip to Port Said, arriving there January 4th. Mr. Dana, who was still in Egypt, met us at the steamer and took us up to Cairo, where he left us to recuperate from our adventures. January 20th saw him and Mr. Glockler back in Beirût. About two hundred Syrians met them at the dock, and Mr. Dana will never forget the numerous touching ways in which his Syrian friends showed their joy at his safe return.

The rest of us remained in Egypt until April. On our return we found Beirût little altered in appearance, but much changed by the occupation. Most striking was the expression of new hope in the faces of the people. We had been at home only a very short time before we began to feel that we had never been away at all. Familiar scenes, familiar faces, and the accustomed work, resumed just where we had left it— these were reality. Constantinople and the year of exile was only a painful dream. And yet, looking back on the experiences of our year and a half of absence, we all feel that, while much of it was trying, it was all worth while.

XV.

THE DARK HOUR BEFORE THE DAWN

THOSE who were in Syria during the year 1918 are agreed that it was the saddest and hardest year of the whole war period. Conditions were steadily growing worse, the powers of resistance had been weakened, and hope was expiring. The end of the war still seemed out of sight, and there were certain indications that it might be months distant. The deportation of Mr. Dana and Rev. W. S. Nelson of the American Mission in Tripoli had so thoroughly alarmed the other Americans that they made themselves as inconspicuous as possible, and for the most part they devoted themselves exclusively to their regular missionary or collegiate activities.

Rev. Paul Erdman of Zaḥleh Station was elected Mr. Dana's successor; and when he left his home in the Lebanon to live in Beirût, he knew that there was a distinct odium attached to the position he was now to occupy, and a possibility that he might share the fate of his predecessor. No one in Beirût knew at that time just what had been the reason for Mr. Dana's deportation, and there was considerable justification for the fear that whoever succeeded him in his work might also be removed by the Government, should he prove too energetic in relief activities. It is impossible to say too much in praise of the way in which Mr. Erdman accepted and discharged the onerous and unfamiliar duties in Beirût, and the courage with which he applied himself to the dangerous task. The circumstances under which he began the work could hardly have been more difficult. Mr. Dana had been in the custody of the Government for the week preceding his sentence to deportation, and was granted only three days in which to close up his business and prepare for departure. It was wholly out of the question to leave his affairs in proper shape to hand them on to any one else. Those last three days he worked day and night, with an average of less than three hours' sleep in twenty-four; but the utmost he could accomplish was to map out roughly the vital principles of policy which should guide his successor. It was impossible for Mr. Erdman to come to Beirût at that time. Consequently, the two men never had an opportunity to discuss the details of the work which the one was handing on to the other under such trying conditions.

Within a few days after Mr. Dana's departure Mr. Erdman was in Beirût. The way in which he handled the difficult situation was nothing short of genius. His only assets, in addition to his own powers, were the " good-will " of the concern he was now directing, and the loyal support of the same corps of assistants that had worked with Mr. Dana. He was obliged, however, to win for himself the confidence of the business men of the city, and to convince them that a

scholar and a teacher—a "mere missionary," as they
might have said—was also a capable man of business.
In his delicate task he succeeded marvellously, and
to-day every business man in Beirût holds Mr. Erdman in high esteem, and praises him both for his
ability and his delightful personality.

The new Manager carried on the work of the Press
along the same lines as before, since he regarded his
administration as merely an interlude, and looked forward to the time when the real Manager would return
to resume his interrupted activities. He made no
changes in policy or practice, continuing as usual the
Syrian remittances and the relief-work. Whatever
alterations he made were slight, and only in concession
to altered conditions. I mention this as an indication
of Mr. Erdman's exquisite tact. It is always easy to
inherit another man's work and alter it in accordance
with one's own judgment, but it is vastly more difficult
to seat oneself at a man's desk and carry on his work
in exactly the way in which he himself would have
done it. It was just that difficult feat which Mr.
Erdman accomplished to perfection; and consequently,
when Mr. Dana returned, he resumed his work as
easily as if he had left it only the night before.

The greatest problem during the last year of the
war was the difficulty of obtaining cash. The Syrian
money-market was extremely limited; and although
Mr. Erdman never let an available sum go by, he could
not secure sufficient funds to finance the work. Mr.
Dana was, fortunately, able to augment Mr. Erdman's
amounts by the sale of his checks in Constantinople

and the transfer of the proceeds to Beirût through regular banking channels. The money-market in Constantinople was less restricted than in Beirût, and the signature of Mr. Dana was already sufficiently familiar there to enable him to negotiate his checks without great difficulties. During the whole time of his absence from Beirût he was able to assist materially in financing the Press and the Mission work in Syria; indeed there were times when it seemed providential that the Mission now had a representative in the Capital, so much greater were the financial opportunities there during this period than in the provinces.

As has been explained already, the only safe mail route for lists and data connected with relief payments was through the State Department in Washington, the American Legation in Stockholm, and the Swedish Minister in Constantinople, and in order to safeguard further the Mission interests, Mr. Dana opened the Press mail in Constantinople. The lists of remittances to Syrians, and correspondence from the New York Treasurer were copied on plain paper, so that in case of another raid on the Press premises in Beirût there would be nothing to indicate that these papers had originated in New York. During seven months of his stay in Constantinople Mr. Dana was in constant touch with his Mission, and even while he was in prison, when Mrs. Dana and I visited him there, he gave me instructions in regard to his business under the very ear of the Turkish censor. He also wrote orders covering relief appropriations which were smuggled out to me, enabling me to secure funds and forward them to Beirût. Thanks to the stupidity of the Turks, although he was in the most closely guarded prison of the Empire, Mr. Dana was able to continue without serious interruption his assistance to the relief effort in Syria.

Mr. Dana was liberated on September 3rd, and at the end of September mail communications between the Capital and Syria were abruptly terminated. About the middle of October we learned of the fall of Beirût, and chafed under our further detention in Turkey when we were longing to take our share in the work of reconstruction and rehabilitation in Syria. It was nearly two months before our release came. On December 1st, Mr. Dana, Dr. Nelson and Mr. Henry Glockler, Mr. Dana's first assistant at the Press, left Constantinople by train *via* Bulgaria, Salonika, and Egypt, *en route* for Beirût.

The conditions in Beirût during our absence we could only surmise; but as we ourselves had lived there through three dreadful years of the war, we did not find it difficult to imagine what the fourth year must have been. During that year the food situation grew steadily worse. Prices soared, and the already greatly depreciated paper-money sank lower in value. Flour, which before the war had sold at four to six piasters per *rotl* for the best grade, could now not be obtained for less than 250 piasters for an inferior quality. In some places the price even went up to 350 piasters ($10.50 for 6 lbs.). There was no employment, no industry, no source of income, except the charity remittances received through the Americans.

Only certain districts in the wheat-belt which had always been practically self-supporting were able to keep up a semblance of their pre-war existence. The population at large was absolutely destitute, and, for the first time during the war, utterly without resources. It was no longer the habitually indigent who were now suffering. That class had been exterminated early in the siege. It was the middle class, those who had formerly been accustomed to modest comfort and decent living, who were now reduced to extremest poverty. The former better-to-do stratum of society, teachers, preachers, small merchants, and landed proprietors were now dependent on charity for their very existence. They had sold every salable object. Household furniture, kitchen utensils, extra clothing and bedding, all had been sacrificed to meet the demand for daily bread. They had economized and scraped along with the barest necessities, and now they had nothing in the world but the clothes on their backs, and a single vessel in which to cook, should they be so fortunate as occasionally to procure the ingredients for a hot meal. Ruined and dismantled houses bore witness to the fact that families in desperation had sold the very roofs from over their heads. The most discouraging feature, from the philanthropic standpoint, was the fact that during this year many families that had been partially supported by relief-funds died—a terrible reminder of the apparent waste and futility of investing money in so feeble a security as human life.

However, the relief-work did continue in a manner

that was surprising, considering the former opposition of the Government. For the first time in three years American charity in Beirût was actually countenanced by the *Vâli*, although he stipulated that it should be carried on in an inconspicuous fashion, and purely under the guise of private philanthropy. The work was modelled after that of the Red Cross in 1914–15, but was very limited in scope. Although the Americans in Syria have always opposed giving relief in the form of money, it was necessary to depart from their ideals at this time, as it was a case of money or nothing. The distribution of food was out of the question owing to the difficulty of transport, and the laws controlling the transfer of supplies from province to province. Furthermore, the *Vâli* had made it very clear that all relief-work must be carried on in an unostentatious manner. A food-distribution, even to a limited number of people, cannot be conducted inconspicuously. The hungry smell it out and throng to the distribution center—then there is the end of charitable attempts, and probably trouble for every one concerned!

There was practically no alteration in the work in Lebanon. The soup-kitchens were enlarged somewhat to meet the increased need, but the limited resources of the Relief Committee and the eternal problem of transportation added greatly to the difficulties connected with their management. It is curious that during this last year, when the Turks might almost be said to have been in sight of success in the extermination of the male population of Syria, they relaxed somewhat their efforts and permitted philanthropic in-

terference more graciously than at any other time during the course of the war. Moreover, the Germans,
who had suggested to the Turks this very policy of
annihilation, now afforded facilities in the matter of
transport that seemed incomprehensible. Perhaps the
explanation is not far to seek. Both Germans and
Turks knew that the end was near. Jerusalem had already fallen on December 9, 1917, and it was only a
question of time until the British forces should take
possession of the whole of Syria. The country had
already been seriously crippled, if not actually drained
of its life-blood. Even the Turks were satisfied with
the success of their plan, and they could now afford
to be magnanimous, especially at a time when their
own fate was extremely precarious. They might yet
be grateful for proofs of good-will toward the country
they had governed, and the foreigners who had been
resident there.

We met so few " typical Germans " in Syria that I
have often wondered whether the German Government sent out here their more humane subjects who
could not be depended upon to play the rôle of " frightfulness " demanded on the Western Front. However
that may be, the German soldier as we encountered
him seemed easy-going, and too sluggish to be ag-
gressively ill-tempered. The drivers of the big freight-
lorries were frequently parties to charitable intrigues,
and seemed equally willing to aid in the rescue of an
orphan girl from a brutal Turkish employer, or in
smuggling grain out of Damascus into Lebanon.
This, however, was purely a matter of personal in-

clination and indicated nothing in regard to the general policy. During the last year of the war even Liman von Sanders, at the instigation of Dr. Dray, authorized the use of German military motor-trucks for the transport of grain into Lebanon for relief purposes, although he stipulated that it should be used only for women and children. Certainly Germany had altered her policy in Syria—I will not say had experienced a change of heart!

Politically a curious state of affairs existed in the country. Jerusalem fell into the hands of the British nearly a year before Damascus and Beirût were captured. The country lived in a state of suspense, therefore, for months after the fall of the Holy City, in the expectation that the army would push on and complete the conquest of Syria. This the enemy failed to do, and by the time that the "big drive" really commenced in the autumn of 1918 the people of Syria were so habituated to the anomalous state of affairs that they had almost forgotten to reckon on the possibility that the British might one day pursue their advance. News of the progress of events in the south filtered through but slowly, and life in the north went on just as when the enemy was more than one hundred and fifty miles away. There was, however, intimate communication between the Arabs east of the Jordan, who were armed and in effective coöperation with the English, and the Druzes of southern Lebanon. In fact, the Arabs with the King of the Hedjaz did their utmost to persuade the Druzes, both in Ḥaurân and Lebanon, to join with them. This the cautious

Druzes refused to do until they were more assured of
the success of the British campaign.   I am told, however, that it was an extremely easy matter to get across
the lines, particularly for an able-bodied Armenian.
In this connection my informant mentioned as one of
the persons who had aided in the escape of a number
of Armenians to the other side an old Arab who had
served as colporteur for the British and Foreign Bible
Society in the Ḥaurân for a number of years.

The Arab party in Syria was gradually assuming
organized form, although political intrigues discovered
by the Turks were so rigorously punished that the
utmost secrecy was necessary.   The fact, however,
that considerable political propaganda was successfully
carried on is proved beyond a doubt by the course of
subsequent events.   When Damascus fell to the Arabs,
the President of the municipality of Beirût received a
telegram ordering him to seize Beirût for the Sherif,
instructions upon which he acted so promptly and effectively as to leave no doubt concerning the complete-
ness of the existent Arab organization.

Apart from their own straightened circumstances,
and the sorrow of the distress about them, the year
1918 was in some ways less wearing for the Americans than the year previous had been.   Every one
lived in fear of an evacuation of the city should the
British advance continue, for the cities of the south,
notably Jaffa, had been evacuated of their civil populations before the enemy's approach.   As the advance
seemed to be arrested for the moment, this fear gradually became intermittent and dependent upon the nature

of rumours from the south. The Government showed no special antagonism toward the Americans during the last few months of its régime in Syria, and the year passed without startling incidents such as had marked 1917. Perhaps the secret of this freedom from annoyance lay in the antagonism which the Turks felt for the Germans. The very fact that the Germans urged a measure was sufficient to make the Turks oppose it with the full force of their authority. It is not evident, however, just what the German attitude was at this time. It is probable that they were too much occupied with their own affairs to care much what the Turks or any one else did. They certainly regarded Turkey as a lost cause. The Turkish army was almost a negligible quantity, and the length of its stay in Syria depended upon the length of time that it took the British Army to make up its mind to move. The final successful British advance caused a perfect stampede among the Germans, and they were the only foreigners in Syria who did not rejoice in that greatest event in the modern history of the country: the British occupation, and the release from the oppression of the Turk.

XVI

DAWN—THE DAY OF SYRIA'S LIBERATION

THE big British drive in Palestine began on
September 19, 1918. The combined German
and Turkish opposition melted away before
the onrush of the enemy, and the flood of occupation
swept northward in three columns, carrying everything before it. The achievements of the Egyptian
Expeditionary Force under the command of that great
general, Sir Edmund Allenby, have already been
chronicled, not only in an elaborate report from official sources published by the *Palestine News,* but also
in a number of very readable personal accounts. It is
not the military side as such that concerns this narrative, but the human side of the drama: how it appeared to those who were in enemy territory, but in
sympathy with the British; and what it meant to Syria.

Probably the most unusual feature of the situation
was the fact that the population of Syria as a whole
was completely in the dark as to the progress of events.
No official report of the enemy's advance, or of the
achievements of the defending army was ever published. The supreme aim of the Turkish military administration was to keep the people in complete ignorance of what was really happening. The only indication of events in the south was the evidence, never

substantiated, of travellers' tales, or the fact that the post and telegraph in Beirût no longer accepted messages for certain places known to be in the path of the British advance. Neither of these channels of information was reliable; in the first place, because rumour ran rife in the country, and every one who was level-headed had long since adopted the attitude of incredulity toward any second-hand item of information; and in the second place, because the government of Beirût frequently severed contact with other parts of the Empire for military reasons, in some cases resuming the interrupted communications after every one had become convinced that this or that city was actually in the hands of the enemy.

Although I was in Constantinople at the time of the fall of Beirût, I have heard the story from one of our community who witnessed that great event. It will always be a tremendous disappointment to me that I was not in Syria myself when this happened, but the joy of returning three months later to a Syria that was no longer Turkish made up in a measure for missing the actual spectacle of the occupation. Whereas those in Syria were entirely ignorant of the near approach of the long-hoped-for release, we in Constantinople followed hour by hour the progress of the advancing forces. Ḥaifâ, Acre, Tiberias, Ammân—one by one we heard of their capture. When the name of Der'â appeared in the dispatches our excitement grew intense. Damascus was the next point of attack; and when that fell, Beirût was as good as taken. When we finally heard that Beirût, our own Beirût, was at last in British possession, we laughed and wept. We knew that the occupation of Syria before the winter set in would mean salvation to thousands in Lebanon, and we were wild with impatience to be back to help in the work of rehabilitation. However, our patience was not put to a very lengthy test. Two weeks later, October 31st, the Turkish Armistice put an end to hostilities on this front. I am not sure now that I would exchange that wonderful experience of seeing the Entente Fleet in the Bosphorus, and the Entente troops in the Capital for even the privilege of being in Beirût on the day of its liberation.

Ten days after the fall of Jerusalem, on December 9, 1917, the event was unofficially reported in Beirût; but it was so persistently denied by the authorities that in time the public came to believe the rumour false. It was some months before the fact of the occupation of Jerusalem became generally accepted in the north. The same was true of the advance in the autumn of 1918. Fragmentary accounts of British successes filtered through, but were usually scouted by the very people who were most willing to believe in their accuracy. On September 19th two members of the faculty of the Syrian Protestant College came independently into possession of facts which, while they did not coincide, convinced these two gentlemen beyond doubt that the " big drive " was on. They spoke of their convictions to their colleagues, but were laughed to scorn. About October 2nd, one of them was so rash as to assert that he believed the British might be in Beirût before College opened on the ninth; but his statement was received with jeers, and one of the other professors asked him to write it down, so that later he might be reminded of his false prediction. The prophet failed to tell me just what he said to this skeptical friend when the British entered the city on October 8th!

The panic among the Germans and Austrians gave the first indication that something was wrong. About the first of October, the German Consul General, who was summering in Brummâna, was summoned by telegram to the city, and he and his family left Brummâna secretly by night. When he reached Beirût he evidently received reassuring news, for he returned to the mountains early the following morning, with the hope that no one had marked his flight. He had been there only two hours when he was again ordered by telegram to flee the country, and he hastily deposited his valuables with friends, and left with his wife and little boy. What route he took subsequently is not known exactly. Some say that he went by carriage to Tripoli (where all his money was stolen from him), and thence by the pass to Ḥoms. Others claim that he merely pretended to take that route, but in reality made a detour around Beirût, returning to the Damascus road, and continuing to Reyâḳ, where he got a train for Constantinople.

The Austrian Vice-Consul and his family made just as precipitous a descent from 'Aleih to Beirût, where they endeavoured to extract from the *Vâli*, Ismail Hakki Bey, the successor of Azmi, a true statement as to the actual necessity for flight. At first the Gov-

ernor refused to admit that there was any cause for
alarm, but finally he advised the distracted official to
leave the country with all possible haste.   In less than
twenty-four hours the Austrians had sold most of their
household effects at auction, and were on their way to
Reyâk.   I must confess that there were some in Beirût
who had suffered from the arrogance and discourtesy
of this Vice-Consul, and who had been offended by
the heartless extravagance of his wife during a time of
extreme suffering in the city, who greatly enjoyed the
sight of them, on top of their baggage, in a German
freight-lorry; and I should be willing to testify from
my own experience that they found this means of
travel far from comfortable.

The German flight from Syria is described by all
witnesses as a perfect stampede.   German morale
seemed to be entirely broken, and fright and the instinct of self-preservation drove the Germans and Austrians to an exhibition of abject terror.   Many German families from Ḥaifâ, and the colonies near Jaffa,
loaded themselves and their possessions into wagons
and drove up along the coast, escaping in some cases
from Beirût northward to Tripoli and Ḥoms, and in
other cases over the mountains to Reyâk.   All were
panic-stricken and demoralized, and each thought only
of himself and fled without even passing on a warning to such of his countrymen as were more ignorant of
the true state of affairs.   Those who kept to the main
roads and finally joined the railway escaped in safety,
but one party which set off northward through the
mountains was killed by the Nusairîyeh north of

Tripoli. This exodus occurred about a week or ten days before the occupation of Beirût, and some days before the fall of Reyâķ; and after that excitement had subsided, Beirût relapsed into its former state of incredulous expectation.

Those who were in the mountains were first warned of the near approach of the British. Dr. Dray, who was in Brummâna, told me the following story:

" On the night of October 5th we were startled by the sound of heavy explosions to the east of us; and we saw the eastern sky illuminated with an awful glow. A heavy mist hung low and served as a screen to reflect the glare of the deadly fireworks, and we could only speculate that the British were bombing Reyâķ from the air. All the next day the heavy cannonading continued, and at night a repetition of the previous night's display.

" My first concern was for the Turkish battery at Beit Meri, which I knew had received orders to bombard Beirût at the first sign of the enemy's approach. This battery was composed of two naval guns from the Turkish warship, the *Hamidiyeh;* and the Turkish naval officer in charge did not understand the military code, nor did his military superior know the naval code. Consequently, all of his orders were telegraphed to him in simple, uncoded messages in Turkish, and were, through the telegraph operators, made known in the village. Furthermore, this Turk was friendly toward me, and himself shared with me such items of military importance as he thought might prove of interest. Through him I learned of the plan to bombard Beirût. I knew that they had the exact range, for a few weeks earlier the Beit Meri battery had indulged in a little target-practice. Four or five tremendous splashes in the sea beyond the city gave evidence of the accuracy of their calculations. I was determined to do my utmost to prevent such a catastrophe as the destruction of Beirût; accordingly, I assembled the head men of the villages in that district and urged them to coöperate with me in an attempt to secure possession of that battery. They were enthusiastic in their support, and we made up quite a little army of civilians and boldly approached the battery. The Turks in command were taken wholly off their guard and attempted no resistance. I parleyed with the officer in command, and told him that as the British were approaching he would best surrender the guns and escape while there was yet time. I finally induced him to give me a list of the pieces in the battery, and of the ammunition, which list I dispatched a few days later to the commander of the Army of Occupation in Beirût, and for which I received official acknowledgment. Our first plan was to disarm the two hundred and fifty Turkish soldiers in charge of the position; but they pled to keep their rifles, as they were certain that if they passed unarmed through the country, they would be massacred by the inhabitants. We finally consented, on condition that they left Beit Meri immediately. I heard later that they went down to the plain, where they surrendered to the first British detachments that arrived.

" One morning we looked down to Beirût, and there

in the harbour lay several warships. From that time onward events occurred so rapidly that I can scarcely recall the exact sequence. On October 8th the British Seventh Division entered Beirût, where they were warmly received, and where some six hundred and sixty Turks, including sixty officers, were surrendered to them by the inhabitants. From our point of vantage on the mountain we watched the progress of a mighty army along the coast. All day long the roads were black with crawling troops, and at night their bivouac fires starred the plain. At daylight they would push on northward, and others would come up during the day to take their places. Within a few days, every village and hamlet in the country quartered British soldiers. In Brummâna, Beit Meri, and the site of the former battery there were seventy-five in all; in other villages ten, or even five Tommies represented the might of the British occupation."

To understand just what conditions existed in the city during those exciting days, we must retrace our steps a bit. About October 1st, the President of the Beirût Municipality, Omar Bey Daouk, on learning of the rapid progress of the British, addressed himself to the Turkish *Vāli* for instructions in case the advance should continue in the direction of Beirût, and the Turkish officials should deem it wisest to leave the city to its fate. The *Vāli* flatly denied that there was any truth in the reports of British successes, and assured Omar Bey that he need not feel the least concern in the matter. Reluctantly, Omar Bey accepted this as a dismissal, and returned home. Excitement in the town, however, grew, and persistent reports of Arab successes greatly agitated and inflamed the Arab sympathizers among the populace.   Once more the President of the Municipality sought the *Vāli*, this time at ten o'clock at night.   When Ismail Hakki persisted in denying that there was any cause for apprehension, Omar Bey became convinced that the Turks were plotting to destroy the city prior to their flight, and his own anxiety was enormously increased.   As he could obtain no information from the *Vāli* there was nothing for him to do but to return home once more. Upon his arrival at his own residence he found a telegram from the Sherîfian party in Damascus announcing the successes in that city, and instructing him to seize Beirût for the King of the Hedjaz.   For a third time Omar Bey sought out the *Vāli*, but this time he went with a strong support of police.   He informed the Turk of the turn events had taken; and announced that, if the *Vāli* were found in the city the following morning, it would be the painful duty of the Municipality to take him prisoner and hand him over to the Army of Occupation when it should enter the city.   The *Vāli*, acting upon this hint, left that night by carriage for Reyâḳ, passing through on his way to Constantinople just three days before the British capture of that town, October 5th.

All that night the President and the Council of the Municipality debated how to enforce order in the town.   The following morning they raised the flag of the Hedjaz over the *Seraiyeh*, or Government Building, and for two days the Administration occupied itself with the institution of a new Moslem government, and new laws appropriate to the occasion. This kept the town interested for a day or two, and the populace was so busy celebrating that it did not show any alarming signs of disorder. On the fourth, a British armoured motor-car entered the city, and was greeted with enthusiasm as a forerunner of the army. In a few hours it left, but the public expectation was that the army would soon put in an appearance. Two days later there were still no signs of a British occupation, and Omar Bey Daouk, fearing disturbances in the city, and even the possible return of the Turks, sent an emissary by sea to Ḥaifâ to beg the British to occupy Beirût. The envoy brought back word that the British would come the next day. All next day they were expected, but failed to put in an appearance; and it was not until the afternoon of the day following, October 8th, that the troops finally began to arrive. The first, a cavalry detachment, came up the coast from Tyre and Sidon; others later moved in from Reyâk over the Lebanon range.

Before the land-forces arrived, five small ships, three French and two British, approached the coast, and the French entered the harbour. The British anchored outside. There were no French troops, but the French marines were permitted to make a demonstration on shore. As soon as the ships had anchored, the President of the Municipality went out to pay his official respects to the British units. That same afternoon the British troops entered the city. Later a small detachment of French who were allowed to share in.

the expedition assisted in the military administration around Beirût.

Thus Beirût once more changed hands, and the beautiful city which had known already so many different masters passed again into the keeping of Christian forces. The country thus liberated from the Turkish yoke was organized under British Military control and administered as " Occupied Enemy Territory." The familiar abbreviation *O. E. T. A.* has come into such general use that it deserves to be included in the next edition of the dictionary! Owing to the fact that Jerusalem had been in British possession so many months before the tide of victory extended to the north and east, there was ample time to organize an effective military administration which could be extended to the territories later conquered. " General Allenby first entrusted the administration of Southern Palestine to his Chief Political Officer, Brigadier-General G. F. Clayton, (C. B., C. M. G.), who built up such measures of government of the civilian populations as are provided for in " The Laws and Usages of War " laid down by the international agreements embodied in the Hague Convention. This administration was entrusted locally to Military Governors. Later the work developed so greatly that in April Major-General Sir Arthur Wigram Money, (K. C. B., C. S. I.), was appointed Chief Administrator of Occupied Enemy Territory Administration, as the control of the administration could no longer be combined with the Political Department. After the successful campaign in the north the Commander-in-Chief found it desirable to divide occupied enemy territory into three sectors, south, north and east. The respective areas were administered under the control of the Commander-in-Chief, by General Money from Jerusalem, by Col. P. de Piepape, C. B. from Beirût, and by Ali Riza Pasha el Rikabi from Damascus." [1]

Those of us who were in the country during the war, find it difficult to believe that we are not dreaming when we see the changes that even a few months of occupation have wrought in the land. Only time can heal the wounds caused by centuries of neglect and by the ravages of a four-year siege; but the day when the first British detachment advanced into Syria, the rehabilitation of the country began. Hope, like the Phœnix, revived from the ashes of despair; and with the liberation from Turkish oppression came the natural human rebound of courage and faith for the future. The British army are welcome guests in the land, and I believe they have learned the meaning of Eastern hospitality. Yet Syria is still in suspense, for her political future has not yet been decided, and until that has been determined there can be no definite progress toward reconstruction or toward effective organization for the future.

[1] "The Advance of the Egyptian Expeditionary Force," published by the *Palestine News.*

XVII

THE NEW DAY

DURING the war the attitude of the average individual toward the eventual signing of peace was distinctly unreasoning. He argued, apparently, that, just as the declaration of war had immediately plunged the whole world into hardships and suffering, so the termination of hostilities would effect an immediate restoration of the happier conditions of pre-war days. The conclusion of peace would bring the world the same instantaneous relief that the extraction of a decayed tooth brings to its suffering possessor. One good sharp pull and all would be over! There were very few who realized that the world was suffering from an abscess which must ripen before the surgeon's knife could prove effective; and that even after the incision had been made, " nature must do the rest," and there would be a slow and painful process of healing during which the whole system must undergo a readjustment. I heard an intelligent young man say only yesterday of the situation in Syria: " The war has been over nearly a year, yet conditions are no better, and in some cases even worse, than they were before the British came." This is perfectly true, and it is no reflection on the British administration which has already wrought marvels of benefit for Syria and Palestine. What is true of Syria is undoubtedly true of other countries the world over.

In Syria to-day the whole theme of national consideration is the Future. The Past we have buried out of sight, and the immediate Present concerns us only in so far as it affects what is to come. Everything hangs in abeyance until that one vital question of Syria's political fate is solved. No one is willing to enter upon any constructive work until he is assured of the destiny of the nation. Everything gives evidence of suspended activity. Only the mind of the nation is keenly alert, and is eager to plumb the unfathomed depths of the future.

What was the future of yesterday is the present of to-day, and during the war it was this very time of which we expected so much. In this respect we have all been disappointed, for we failed to take into calculation the length of time which must be spent in convalescence. The world has been mortally ill, and once the crisis is past it cannot rise immediately from its bed and resume the activities of normal health. Syria has lain at the point of death, and there were times when it seemed incredible that she should ever rally. She has drawn to the limit upon her physical resources, and it will take a long time to renew her exhausted powers.

A year ago we prayed for the occupation, and we dared not face the inevitable and terrible tragedy that must certainly ensue if no relief came before winter. The autumn brought liberation from the Turk; but no military occupation, however welcome and beneficent, can free a country from the consequences of the inexorable physical laws of the universe. Moreover, the occupation of Syria, and even the signing of peace with Germany, do not yet mean the end of the war. Armies are still mobilized, and are in the field in Russia and Afghanistan. Internal conditions all over the world indicate national unrest; and the traveller who must submit to endless red-tape in the matter of visés, permits, *etc.*, realizes that a state of war still exists even after hostilities have technically terminated. The British occupation of Syria in the autumn proved the salvation of vast numbers during the following winter; but one of the greatest fallacies, both at home and abroad, is the assumption that, because the Turk has been driven out of the country and the Entente has taken possession, Syria can now be regarded as amply provided for, and is no longer in need of assistance from outside.

Before touching on the subject of primary importance to all those who love Syria and are interested in her welfare, let me first explain what I mean by saying that Syria has hardly begun to recover from the effects of the war, and that she still needs all the sympathy, coöperation, and philanthropy which have been accorded her during the past four years. The most striking illustration of Syria's need which occurs to me is the simile that some one used recently in a discussion of this very problem. He was pleading for continued American relief support, and he said: "As soon as a child learns to take its first step do we expect that it will thenceforth be able to walk alone without further assistance from parents or nurse?" Perhaps it would be even more pertinent to inquire, whether a man who is too poor to provide himself with medicines or with the delicacies of invalid diet, should forgo charitable assistance as soon as he is able to partake of solid food? What about the expensive dainties which he must have to enable him to recover his strength?

The whole world has been hard hit by the war, and there are certain regions which have suffered more than others. So great is the distress in some localities that American philanthropy has been forced to confine its support to the cases of most desperate need. The Caucasus still needs millions of dollars of American money; and if one believes the reports, even millions are hardly more than a drop in the bucket. In Syria, however, a few hundred thousands will go a long way, and will prove the salvation of numbers of intelligent and worthy citizens. One of the members of the American Relief Committee in Beirût was requested by the Committee to prepare a careful survey of actual conditions in the country at the present time, with suggestions as to how best to meet the need. His findings may be summarized as follows:

During the winter that is ahead of us (1919–20) there will be an appalling number of families in *great* distress. They are without houses, without bedding, without a change of clothing, without a single cooking utensil, and have absolutely no resources with which to procure the barest necessities. They have already sold everything they possess. They have worried along during the summer while they could live out-of-doors, when a single garment sufficed as a concession to decency, while there were fruits and vegetables to be had for the asking, and while a cooked meal was not indispensable. But how are they going to face the winter? They have neither shelter, food, nor clothing. There is no work, for the industries of the country have not yet been resumed, and cannot be for some time to come. These people are not the habitually indigent, but may be described as the upper lower class. The lowest class, representing the paupers of war-days, is now better off than its social superiors. It exists in a state of animal contentment. The work of public improvements, which was suspended during the period of the war, has provided employment for the physically fit, the day-labourer. The wages which repay his exhausting drudgery suffice to keep him and his family in food, and he is not inconvenienced by cultivated instincts which demand luxuries, or comforts, or any of the refinements of life. For the moment, the army provides employment for the men of what we might call the educated class; and as interpreters, and clerks, they are well paid. There remains still a social stratum midway between these two, comprising those who have learned to live respectably, who cannot go in rags, or beg, and who are not physically capable of the type of manual work which provides for the day-labourer. For the sake of outward respectability these people have provided themselves with decent clothing, even though they have had to go without food to do so. They cannot hold out much longer. Death is ahead, but they face it bravely, and without complaint. They are too proud to solicit charity, and yet they are the very ones who, for the sake of the country, should be saved for future usefulness.

Leaving out of account the better-to-do classes of society—merchants, business and professional men—and confining our attention to the two lower strata we find that the lowest, or pauper class, is at present provided for. There is a second class of tens of thousands of deserving and desirable citizens who must perish unless they receive immediate assistance, but who can be set on their feet by a comparatively small outlay. If this class of people can be equipped with the bare necessities of life, and provided with employment, they will soon be capable of self-support.

The one thing that prevents Syria from rising unaided to her feet is the fact that there is no possible means by which she can provide employment for all who must work to live. For the past few months, and for a few months yet to come, there has been employment for a limited number of able-bodied men in necessary forms of work which were deferred during the war, but which must now be continued. This includes the building and repair of roads, repairs and alterations on public buildings, completion of houses started before the war but never finished, repairs on walls, property, *etc.* But all these things will eventually be finished; and until the political fate of Syria is settled nothing new will be commenced. Even the fact that the population has decreased by nearly fifty per cent. only partially contributes toward solving the problem of labour. While there are fewer men to compete for employment, on the other hand, there are certain industries which have been completely destroyed, or so crippled that they can no longer provide for the numbers that they supported before the war. For instance, the silk industry for which Syria was once famous, and which proved a source of tremendous income, is now destroyed. The mulberry trees, the leaves of which provide the one item of the silkworm's diet, have either been cut down for fuel or have been so damaged by mistreatment and neglect that the leaves are no longer good for silkworm cultivation. It was hoped that after the war, when it would be possible to secure good eggs from Europe, the industry would revive, but this injury to the trees is a handicap which only time can correct. All over the country the silk factories have been dismantled, and in some cases completely destroyed. The rehabilitation of the silk industry will require years, and of course, considerable capital. What is true of this industry is true also of others.

The Lebanon Mountains, always sparsely forested, are rapidly becoming denuded. During the war the Turks and the Germans felled the trees for fuel on the railways, and to-day the British lorries are carrying hundreds of tons from the pitiful little forests in the mountains. This loss of timber will eventually affect the climate, and even where young trees have already started, it will be decades before the forests can be restored.

The only hope for the country, therefore, lies in assistance from the outer world. Foreign capital must contribute toward developing its natural resources; and trade with Europe, America and South America must rehabilitate the depleted finances of this impoverished land. It will be seen, therefore, why it is that Syria is awaiting with impatience the decision in Paris in regard to her national status. Syria herself realizes that she is not at present in a condition for self-government, and her one desire is for protection and guidance under an acceptable mandate. There are many indications that Syria deserves to be consulted in regard to her destiny. Less than a year has elapsed since the departure of the Turk, but in that year changes have taken place in the country that are almost unbelievable to one who knew it at the lowest ebb of its existence. During the Ottoman régime there was no political cohesion among the Syrians. Racial and sectarian disagreements were paramount over national considerations, and the true patriot despaired, doubting whether anything could weld together these antagonistic factions. The curse of Syria has always been the religious fanaticism of her various sects. The increasing nationalistic tendency of to-day is, therefore, by far the most hopeful sign that Syria possesses latent elements of strength, and a spark of that divine fire which, if properly fostered, will flame into national enthusiasm and patriotism.

There is only one topic of conversation in all Syria

to-day, and that is the political fate of the country. Moslem, Druze, and all sects of Christians, with but one notable exception, are united in their demand for an undivided Syria under an acceptable mandate. They have very positive ideas as to what would be an acceptable mandatory power. The choice lies between two nations, England and America. The findings of the Commission appointed by the Peace Conference to study the public sentiment of Syria, which visited us in the summer of 1919, show an overwhelming majority in favour of the United States, with England as an acceptable alternative. It is probably not included in the report of the Commission, but it is a well-known fact in the country that any other arrangement for the political future of Syria will result in bloodshed and in a duplication of the Balkan problem.

Syria is only one of the many small nations that has staked her future on America's good faith in abiding by President Wilson's " Fourteen Points," and so great is Syria's confidence in America's loyalty to principle that she is willing to entrust her national existence into our keeping. The President of the United States has given utterance to principles of justice which offer a hope of salvation to all national units that have been the victims of political oppression and injustice, and Syria understands the principles which America stands for and is willing to accept her guardianship.

On the other hand, she admires and respects Great Britain, and sees all about her the beneficent results of British rule in Egypt and India. She is confident that as a British protectorate she likewise would flourish. The question yet to be answered, however, is whether Britain can assume any further responsibilities than those she has already shouldered, and whether she will be willing to accept another charge. Britain already bears a resemblance to the Old Woman Who Lived in a Shoe, and she may feel that she has her hands quite full enough as it is.

There is one arrangement, however, for Syria's future which will never be acceptable to the people, and that is a settlement which will necessitate the division of her territory. Fear of such a contingency has frequently given rise to the rumour that Palestine was to be constituted a separate state under a separate administration, Damascus another, and northwestern Syria (enlarged Lebanon) yet a third. Great has been the national lamentation wherever this report has been given credence. The slogan of the nationalistic party is first and foremost " Syria undivided." Any refusal of this demand will lead to unrest, and in time to bloodshed, unless the cause of dissatisfaction be removed. France's commercial interests have led her diplomats to hope that Syria's choice might be accorded to her; but, except for a portion of the Maronite sect, there is no enthusiasm for France, especially since her economic condition is not such as to enable her to undertake the rehabilitation of such an impoverished country.

The question uppermost in the minds of those who are interested in the Syrian problem is undoubtedly this: Is Syria capable of self-government even under a mandatory power? It is true that her apparent weakness under Turkish administration may argue her unfitness for political responsibility. There seems to be only one answer to that objection, namely, that the character of Turkish control was such as to crush the heart out of every subject race. What has been true of Syria was true of Egypt before the British intervention, was true also of the Balkan provinces of Turkey before they attained their independence, was true of Armenia as well. One has only to observe results when a Syrian is removed from his Turkish *milieu* to a more stimulating environment. Look at the Syrian in Egypt. Every one who knows anything about the Near East knows that he has succeeded. Kitchener is said to have asserted that but for the educated Syrians in the country, Egypt would be forty years behind her present position. The Syrians are among the most influential men in that land. They hold positions second only to the British in importance. In politics, in business, in social life the Syrian community of a city like Cairo is sound to the core, and is an example to the Egyptians that they might well follow.

In America the Syrians have an excellent record. I have been told that police statistics in a city like New York rate them among the lowest in the average of crime. They take to business like ducks to water; and as far as my experience has gone with Syrian business men from America, they are honest, thrifty, and loyal to our Government. One of them, whom I now number among my acquaintances here, was actually mayor of his town in the United States. This has been true not merely of exceptional individuals, but of the race as a whole, and therefore it is not a great strain on the imagination to assume that, if the Syrians can make good citizens abroad, they can make good citizens at home if given a proper chance. When the fate of the country is once decisively settled, it is to be hoped that the Syrians overseas will be animated by patriotic responsibility, and that each will do his share to help his native land. Some may best serve the interests of their country by returning there to live. Others may prove more serviceable where they are, but it will not be in keeping with the Syrian character as I understand it if they fail to support their nation to the very limit of their resources in so important a crisis of its history.

If, on the other hand, Syria's right to self-determination is disregarded, and the nation is forced under an administration that is generally unpopular, it is a foregone conclusion that the most desirable types of Syrian citizens will emigrate to other countries. They have suffered too long under a pernicious system of government to risk remaining in the country under such baneful circumstances. Then indeed is Syria doomed!

The present crying need is a complete reorganization of the administration, and the removal from office of those local officials who served under the Turks, and who have been allowed by the *O. E. T. A.* to remain in office. They are, almost without exception, "grafters" and "crooks." In the day of the Turk they abused their power and preyed upon the people. To-day the same men, or men of the same spirit, conduct the administration along Turkish lines. Syria needs a political house-cleaning, and she has a right to demand that the power of the country should be entrusted to those who are fit to govern, and not to the worst type of political " boss."

Does America realize the status of Syria to-day? The Syrians represent the highest type of culture and intelligence in the Arabic-speaking world, which comprises one-fifteenth of the population of the globe. They are born to be leaders of the Arab race, and that means not merely the inhabitants of Syria and Arabia, but also of Africa, India, Persia, and hundreds of colonies in islands of the East, in South America, and in the United States. They might almost be considered the leaven of the Orient. The Arab world of the future must look to the Syrian race, which is capable of such great cultural development, for its leaders in science, philanthropy, and politics, and for the statesmen who alone can master the complicated problems of Pan-Arabia. There is no country in the world open to American influence where such far-reaching results can be obtained as through an American mandate over Syria. Here is a nation of perhaps two million people capable of developing into the finest type of world-citizens, awakened to a sense of responsibility, and to a patriotic enthusiasm, clamouring for the right to live a peaceful and honourable life. If Syria turns to America with a prayer for assistance shall we lend a deaf ear? Shall we condemn her to exploitation by unscrupulous Powers who have no interest in her welfare, but who labour only for their own selfish ends? Shall we abandon those glorious "Fourteen Points" at the first test of their sincerity? Or shall we use all our influence to see that Syria gets justice?

Life in Syria is at a standstill until this vital question is answered. If England agrees to assume a protectorate, as in Egypt, all will be well, and a new era of national prosperity and enthusiasm will open up. The Syrians know and understand the British rule as they see it in the countries that are their nearest neighbours, and they will welcome a British mandate. It only rests with England to determine whether she can add this to the many burdens she already bears.

Or shall it be a self-governing Syria under American guidance, with the backing of America's vast wealth, her systems of justice, tolerance, and education? America, no less than England, will be acceptable as a disinterested friend, with no political ambitions in this part of the world, who has laid aside her national exclusiveness for the sake of lending a hand to a sister-nation that is in desperate need of aid.

The time for the decision cannot be far distant, and for the sake of Syria, we all hope that her fate may soon be determined. There is a faint light in the sky which gives promise of the coming dawn. This gray glimmer has been visible for some time, and the impatient watcher wonders what has happened to delay the sun. Every one knows how wearisome is such an interval of suspense. Light has come, but it is still too early to tell whether the sun will rise clear and fair, or whether he will be veiled in clouds.   We are watchers before the dawn in Syria, but we do not yet know whether our day is to be one of sunshine or of storm.

EXTRAORDINARY WAR PRICES IN SYRIA AND CONSTANTINOPLE, 1917-18

Article	*Amt.*	*Pre-war price*	*Extreme price in dollars*
Beans	1 ℔.	$ .04½	$0.75
Belting for dress...	1 yd.	.09	.95
Blankets, cotton, crib	1	.80	9.00
Candles ....each		.04½	.36
Caning a chair.....	1	.80	12.00
Charcoal ....100 ℔s.		1.15	9.00
Chocolate, sweet....	1 cake	.21	2.10
Coffee	1 ℔.	.23	6.00
Cotton, absorbent...	50 gms.	.18	1.20
" flannel	1 yd.	.13	1.95
" muslin	1 yd.	.13	4.05
" spool .....600 yds.		.05¾	5.00
Cream of tartar....	1 ℔.	.09	1.80
Eggs ....each		.01	.45
Elastic for garters..	1 yd.	.11	2.40
Embroidery cotton..	1 skein	.04½	.72
Flour	6 ℔s.	.15	10.50
Hats, straw, untrimmed		.80	7.50
Honey	1 ℔.	.14	1.20
Kerosene	9 gals.	1.80	180.00
" retail	1 cupful		1.20
Macaroni	1 ℔.	.05	1.05
Machine needles....each		.03	.22
Matches, safety.....	1 small box	.09(doz.)	.15 each
Milk	1 qt.	.05	2.40
Milk, Nestle's.......	1 tin	.35	7.50 in Aleppo
Medicines:			
Alcohol	1 qt.		1.60
Cod Liver Oil....	1 bottle		8.25
Cuticura Oint....	1 box		1.20
Epsom Salts......	1 case	22.50	1500.00 Bid, held for higher bid
Eye dropper......	1 glass		1.20
Glycerine	30 gms.		.50
Iodine	30 gms.		.30
Lysol	1 smallest size		1.05
Toothpaste	1 small tube		1.50
Tooth brush......	1		1.20
Quinine	2 grain tablet		1.50

Article	Amt.	Pre-war price	Extreme price in dollars
Molasses, Native...	1 ℔.	.16	1.05
Mosquito net.......	1	4.00	24.00
Nails, large.........	1 ℔.	.20	7.50
Olive Oil...........	1 qt.	.14	1.05
Onions, dried.......	1 ℔.	.03	.40
Razor blades.......	1 doz.	1.60	4.50
Rice	1 ℔.	.05	1.50
Salt, rock..........	6 ℔s.	.06	.90
" table	1 ℔.	.02	1.50
Soap, laundry......	1 cake	.08	.60
" toilet	1 cake	.10	2.40
Shaving Soap.......	1 cake	.10	.60
Shoes, men's.......	1 pr.		78.00
" women's ...	1 pr.		45.00
" child's	1 pr.		15.00
Stockings, women's.	1 pr. lisle		7.50
Silk socks, men.....	1 pr.		2.55
Socks, cotton, child's	1 pr.		1.75
Silk	1 yd.	1.50	24.00
Soda	1 ℔.	.15	4.20
Starch, laundry.....	1 ℔.	.22	6.00
Sugar	1 ℔.	.06	4.50
Sweater, worsted...	1		15.00
" silk	1		75.00
Tea	1 ℔.	.80	12.75
Tin bowl, 28"......		.50	4.60
Towels, small bath.	1		3.00
Turkey, alive.......	15 ℔s.	4.50	13.50
Typewriter ribbon..	1	.50–.75	20.00
Underwear, woolen.	1 suit		30.00
" gauze .	1 shirt	.35	3.75
" child's gauze	1 shirt	.20	2.40
Woolen suitings....	1 yd.	2.00	36.00
" overcoat ..	1 man's	15.00	145.00 minimum
" " ..	1 ladies'	15.00	75.00 "

N. B.—Most of the prices quoted are for Beirût. Constantinople prices do not differ much from those in Syria at the same time.

Folios Archive Library

The Caliphs' Last Heritage: A Short History of the Turkish Empire
Lt. Col. Sir Mark Sykes

644pp • 218 x 135 mm • Paper £12.95 • ISBN 1 85964 168 7

Newmarket and Arabia: An Examination of the Descent of Racers and Coursers
Roger D. Upton

228pp • 198 x 135 mm • Paper £12.95 • ISBN 1 85964 162 8

The Thistle and the Cedar of Lebanon
Habeeb Risk Allah Effendi

416pp • 202 x 120 mm • Paper £12.95 • ISBN 1 85964 163 6

The Land of Uz
Abdullah Mansûr (G. Wyman Bury)

392pp • 215 x 138 mm • Paper £14.95 • ISBN 1 85964 121 0

Arabia Infelix: Or the Turks in Yamen
G. Wyman Bury

232pp • 215 x 138 mm • Paper £14.95 • ISBN 1 85964 122 9

Narrative of the Residence of Fatalla Sayeghir among the Wandering Arabs of the Great Desert
Collected and translated by M. Alphonse de Lamartine

216pp • 210 x 120 mm • Cased £19.95 • ISBN 1 85964 088 5

The Land of the Date
C. M. Cursetjee

208pp • 235 x 168 mm • Cased £30.00 • ISBN 1 85964 038 9

The History of the Wahabis from their Origin until the End of 1809
Louis Alexandre Olivier de Corancez

224pp • 235 x 168 mm • Cased £25.00 • ISBN 1 85964 036 2

Mount Lebanon: A Ten Years' Residence
Colonel Charles Henry Churchill

Vols. 1–3 • 400pp • 235 x 158 mm • Cased £30.00 • ISBN 1 873938 50 0
ISBN 1 873938 51 9 • ISBN 1 873938 52 7

Mount Lebanon: The Druzes and the Maronites under the Turkish Rule
Colonel Charles Henry Churchill
Vol. 4 • 300pp • 235 x 158 mm • Cased £30.00 • ISBN 1 873938 53 5

Southern Arabia
Theodore and Mabel Bent
504pp • 235 x 168 mm • Cased £45.00 • ISBN 1 85964 035 4

The Countries and Tribes of the Persian Gulf
Colonel Samuel Barrett Miles
644pp • 235 x 168 mm • 4 engravings • Cased £45.00 • ISBN 1 873938 56 X

Travels through Arabia and other Countries in the East
Carsten Niebuhr
212 x 125 mm • Cased £30.00
Vol. I • 464pp • 10pp engravings, 2 maps • ISBN 1 873938 43 8
Vol. II • 456pp • 10pp engravings, 1 map • ISBN 1 873938 54 3

Travels of Ali Bey in Morocco, Tripoli, Cyprus, Egypt, Arabia, Syria and Turkey
235 x 168 mm • Cased £30.00
Vol. I • 383pp • 44 engravings, 2 maps • ISBN 1 873938 39 X
Vol. II • 388pp • 38 engravings, 4 maps • ISBN 1 873938 40 3

Notes on the Bedouins and the Wahabys
John Lewis Burckhardt
Vol. I • 400pp • 235 x 168 mm • Cased £30.00 • ISBN 1 873938 26 8
Vol. II • 400pp • 235 x 168 mm • Cased £30.00 • ISBN 1 873938 32 2

Sinai, the Hedjaz and the Soudan
James Hamilton
440pp • 235 x 168 mm • 1 plate, 1 map • Cased £45.00 • ISBN 1 873938 38 1

A Voyage up the Persian Gulf
Lieutenant William Heude
252pp • 235 x 168 mm • 4 engravings • Cased £45.00 • ISBN 1 873938 44 6

Gazetteer of the Persian Gulf, Oman and Central Arabia
John Gordon Lorimer
10,000pp • 237 x 168 mm • Cased 19-volume set £3,000.00 • ISBN 1 85964 127 X

Contact our Sales Department on +44 (0)118 959 7847 or e-mail on **orders@garnet-ithaca.demon.co.uk** to order copies of these books.